The Other Side
—— *of* ——
Communication

Junior

JEAN VAUTOIR PAUL

jean.paul751@yahoo.com
(561) 283-9867

ISBN 978-1-0980-9217-7 (paperback)
ISBN 978-1-0980-9218-4 (digital)

Copyright © 2021 by Jean Vautoir Paul

All rights reserved. No part of this publication may be reproduced, distributed, or transmitted in any form or by any means, including photocopying, recording, or other electronic or mechanical methods without the prior written permission of the publisher. For permission requests, solicit the publisher via the address below.

Christian Faith Publishing, Inc.
832 Park Avenue
Meadville, PA 16335
www.christianfaithpublishing.com

Printed in the United States of America

This book is dedicated to my wonderful wife Yvonie Paul, who has been everything to me—my love, my adviser, my counselor, the mother of my children, etc. She's always there for me no matter what the circumstances may be in life. "I love you, honey." And I also dedicate this book to my three awesome and beautiful daughters (Bianka Paul, Nakysha Paul, and Mycaina Paul) who have been very good to their parents, themselves, and other people around them. "Positive parents, positive kids." They make us so proud, and we couldn't ask for more. That's exactly how it goes down when we put God first in our family and everything else second. "Families that pray together stay together." There is no other way to do it. No matter what we went through, we always feel blessed, and that's why we stuck with one another and stay as a real family. Thank you, God. And I also dedicate this book to my bishop Don McDougal, from the Church of Jesus Christ of Latter-day Saints, who was always there for us during our hardship or deprivation in our lives. May God continues to bless you and your family abundantly! The Paul family loves you very much.

Let us talk with compassion and understanding to one another!

Let us talk with respect to one another. It is everything!

Let us bring less pain and suffering to our brothers and sisters!

Let us put God first in everything that we do!

A positive person is someone who is able to catch every single rock that life throws at him, and build a solid foundation for his future.

My rolling stone is positivity. What's yours?

CONTENTS

Introduction 13

Chapter 1: Healthy Communication vs. Unhealthy
　　　　　　Communication 17
Chapter 2: Healthy vs. Unhealthy Marriages and Relationships 76
Chapter 3: Parenting at Its Best 117
Chapter 4: Domestic Violence 163
Chapter 5: How to Love and Be Loved 185

Conclusion 223

INTRODUCTION

My name is Jean Vautoir Paul. And thank God for that day, it's finally here. All my life, I always wanted to be an influential author and a role model so I can influence and motivate others to do the right thing and believe in themselves. Therefore, I thought about writing influential and educational books, but never took the time to do so. One day, I woke up and said to myself, "Today is the day to start." I took my pen because I couldn't afford a computer, and I thought very deeply and wrote down thirty tittles that I dream to turn into thirty influential and educational books. Hopefully, I will write all of them before I die; and I know, with the grace of God, everything is possible. Here are a few tittles: "The Other Side of Communication," "Dysfunctional Families," "Choose Kindness," "An Attitude of Gratitude," "A World of Deception," "Self-Destruction of Today's Inner-City Teens," "Happiness Is a Choice, Haiti Mother of Freedom," and the list goes on and on.

My goal in life is to help and motivate other people to better their lives in every corner or area of it when it comes to positivity and do the right thing, make people feel good about themselves, and take them to the other side of communication so they can learn how to communicate with themselves and others more effectively and compassionately. As human beings, we suffer from a disease called; "negativity syndrome" that is destroying our happiness, health, marriages, relationships, careers, communication, etc. Therefore, I came up with an antidote to cure such disease—Vautoir's antidote—which I am willing, ready, and able to share with everybody so together we can fight this pandemic call "negativity."

Every single day, I live my life with constant fear.

- Fear that the day might go by without treating someone the way that I would like to be treated.
- Fear that the day might go by without helping someone who needs help.
- Fear that the day might go by without treating someone with respect.
- Fear that the day might go by without communicating with compassion and understanding with someone.
- Fear that the day might go by without being the best parent that I can be.
- Fear that the day might go by without helping the less fortunate.
- Fear that the day might go by without expressing my gratitude to God and my wife.
- Fear that the day might go by without showing someone that I really care.
- Fear that the day might go by without listening deeply to someone in pain and suffering.
- Fear that the day might go by without showing love and kindness to my surroundings.
- Fear that the day might go by without helping a negative person to see the bright light of positivity.
- Fear that the day might go by without putting a smile on someone's face.

These are twelve components of Vautoir's wall of "good intentions" that I am sharing with my readers because I would like to see each and every one of you stay on the right corner of life so you can treat yourselves and others better and accomplish greatness.

This is my real agenda in life because my mission on earth is based on this agenda. It was about time for me to start this wonderful mission. Hopefully, I will inspire a lot of people, especially my readers, when it comes to communicating with themselves and others while staying in a positive mood.

According to my research, "Communication is the process of passing information and understanding from one person to another. In simple words it's a process of transmitting and sharing ideas, opinions, facts, values etc. from one person to another or one organization to another." In this book, I take communication a little bit farther. I even turn it upside down so my readers can be very knowledgeable when it comes to communication and find themselves on the other side of it.

The Other Side of Communication is a book that talks about the importance of communication. And it also teaches how many branches that communication has. It shows how important to communicate with others and ourselves (self-taught) and how to do just that. It talks about the importance of communication in marriages and relationships, family relationships, coworker relationships, domestic violence, and so forth. It also talks about the kind of food that we should nourish our bodies, minds, and souls with. I use the word *food* because when it comes to communication, it's also a kind of food that we consume every day. We listen to others talking. We watch TV. We go to the movies, and we write about things. We talk about things that can heal us or kill us, things that can be healthy or unhealthy; and these things can be very toxic for us mentally, physically, emotionally and spiritually.

This book also differentiates healthy from unhealthy communication, healthy from unhealthy relationships so my readers can have a better understanding when it comes to good and bad communication and relationships. It also teaches the importance of wisdom, understanding and compassion toward others, and our moral values that is slipping away from us day by day. This book will put my readers in a "mindful of awareness" or "self-awareness," in other words, make sure that the mind-set of my readers is stable and solid when it comes to healthy communication and relationships. This book teaches also how to think before talking because it will take each one of you very deep inside of you (breathe-in-breathe-out moment) so you can be aware of what to say, what not to say before you can engage a conversation with anyone. It will put each of my readers in an awareness mode so they can be in the know zone of what is within them and their surroundings. It talks about how to love and to be loved which is vital to each and every human being living on this earth because it's a "must" to know how to love in order to be loved so we can live happily ever after. This work will push everyone that reads it from the back to move forward with a speed of 100 miles per/ hour so they can live their lives accordingly when it comes to love, "relationships, marriages, communication, etc.

Most of us are disconnected with ourselves because not once we take time to talk to ourselves (self-talk) by asking ourselves important, valuable, and positive questions. In communication, we find what we call emotions, self-esteem, compassion, and self-confidence. Such book raises the bar of these components and teaches my readers the right way of thinking and talking, when it comes to having a conversation, and communicating with anyone or group, for sure. It comes with an antidote, "Vautoir's antidote," that has the power to ease pain and suffering and heal the emotions, concerns, anger, negative attitudes and behaviors. It will better relationships, guide my readers to effective or healthier communication, and teach them how to become the best parents that they can be. This "Vautoir's antidote," is also against "pollution and dangerous toxins" that's coming out of the mouths of negative people. It's all about "pollution solution," so I can protect communication around the world so we can live "pollution free" when it comes to communicating with one another.

Therefore, sit tight and fasten your seatbelt for this awesome and smooth ride to the other side of communication.

CHAPTER 1

Healthy Communication vs. Unhealthy Communication

Brothers and sisters, good and effective communication is the ability to convey messages, even negative ones, in a positive manner. Positive communication has the power to convert negative feelings into positive ones and can help anybody to create a positive impression for himself. Be aware, any positive or healthy communication will elicit positive effects on the other person that you are talking to or having a conversation with by the way they respond to you or even by their actions. When you are trying to have a healthy communication, please do everything in your power to avoid negative or unhealthy statements. Avoid to use words like "I'm unable," "I can't do it," "It is impossible," etc., in your conversation. You can always build your sentences in a manner that contains no negative words but still have the same meaning. For example, instead of saying that "it is impossible for me to succeed in life," it will be better and helpful to say, "If I don't put certain time and effort in what I need to do to succeed, it won't be easy." It will be more difficult for me to get where I want to be.

Healthy communication is the heavy-duty machine that can destroy and bring down the barrier of miscommunication and build the wall of diversity and understanding. Communication is a very powerful tool that can be used to flip workplaces, relationships, marriages, friendships, etc. With effective communication, you will bring trust and understanding to any problem that you may facing. I know it seems more likely to be easy to say than done, but know this with positivity, you can accomplish anything in life because the real power which is the power to convert sits right in the hands of positive communication. There is no better and greater feeling, brothers and sisters, when you can create a positive impression for yourself.

In life, most things or people we encounter in our lives or on our path are loaded with negative elements. It's up to us to make the most of it. What do I mean by that? What I mean is that I want you to look only at the positive aspects because every negative thing has a positive side of it. Believe it or not, all you have to do is flip it, best strategy ever. When you act in such positive manner or have such positive attitude, you just keep yourself happy, your heart smiling and healthy. I know, you know, they know, and we all know that a positive attitude will help one with his career succeed. Brothers and sisters, my suggestion to you would be to start writing down positive conversation that you would have with someone and start using them in verbal communication with friends, family members, even strangers, and score yourselves to see how you did just like I did. It works for me.

I guarantee you that this method will help you a lot and your positive attitude will take you to places where you never imagine that it would take you. It will even ship your career to another level; that's the real positive side and positive aspects of communication—if you are only a positive person that only says positive things to yourself and others, read positive or knowledgeable books only, watch good and positive things on TV, if there's any! That's the best nutritious food that somebody can feed their brain. It means also that such individual is digesting things in his mind that can grow his understanding and compassion, which I will define later. Most of the time, we engage in conversations that make us insecure or feel bad about ourselves, even make us think that we are better and superior to others. Please reject these brain-killer thoughts and feelings. It's like opening your door to the devil; think about it. A positive mind is what requires to let go negative thoughts and feelings. Mindfulness is a necessary ingredient in a positive communication. It takes you to a journey deep inside of you so you can be aware of what to say and what not to say (positive vibes). Therefore, it puts you on your tiptoes so you can know what is within you and your surroundings (being alert). It also pushes you to ask yourself a very important question: is what I'm thinking right this minute healthy or toxic for my mind? With such attitude, you can only think and act positively.

The thoughts you produce as human beings should be healthy to you and others. A positive conversation or the way that we communicate to each other will determine if you are a compassionate or an unkind individual. Communication is a source of nourishment because as humans, we always search for someone to communicate with. But the conversation that we choose to have with our friends, family members, or strangers can be very healthy or unhealthy.

Be aware or stay alert of people that you are talking or surrounding yourself with. It would be wise to engage only healthy conversations so you can go easy on your health. In order to do just that, you need to surrender yourself with positive people only; and by doing that, you will keep rolling the dice of positive communication. And that is the only way that you will see the other side of communication. You have to have enough positivity or be mindful of awareness within you in order not to soak up these deadly diseases. When you talk with compassion and positivity, you only protecting yourself and others from toxic conversation. Mindfulness is also an act of producing compassion and positivity through other people around you and wherever you go. In other words, it means that positivity and compassion protect you and push you so hard so you can live your life accordingly.

As human beings, most of us don't think before talking with others. It can be our romantic partner, husband, wife, family members, friends, coworkers, etc. What we don't understand and don't want to understand is that once we launch those toxic and harsh words, we can't take them back because they already cause the damage. They will leave wounds that will never heal, will never erase the in-and-out scar of the victim, and will be for eternity. Most people that I know that went through verbal abuse or toxic communication always let such anomaly drag down to the mud their personality, moral ethic, dignity, and integrity. What had been said to the victim can be very noxious and damaging and can even cause stress and depression. Studies have proven that "stress can have a lasting negative impact on the brain. Toxic or unhealthy communication and conversation can bring a lot of stress. Even a few days of stress can do great damage to the neurons inside of the hippocampus the area of the brain that allow us to reason and memorize things. So weeks of stress cause reversible damage to neuronal dendrites (the small 'arms' that brain cells use to communicate with each other), and months of stress can permanently destroy neurons. Stress is a formidable threat to your success when stress gets out of control, your brain and your performance suffer."

Toxic or unhealthy communication can force our brain to have a stress response at a very high level. It's in everyone best interest to avoid toxic people at all cause. If we take a good look at the word *toxic*, we can only see poison. Therefore, we can say that a toxic communication can be "poisonous" for our mind, body, and soul. It can be very damaging for our health and relationships. We communicate to each other at very disrespectful levels so we really need to control our anger and don't let our temper make us say or do negative things. Let us be "mindful" about what we really want to say. We need to get in the habit of putting together our thoughts and run after them until we catch them and put them to use in a positive way. The way that some of us communicate to others tell people who we really are. It tells them about our personality and have a huge impact on how they conceive and what they think of us. When we use positive communication phrases, others think that we are positive and respectful people. In contrast, when we use negative communication to communicate or talk with others, people see us as ignorant and rude individuals. Positive communication helps us to connect with others. It also helps us to speak clearly, effectively, and directly to other people. When talking or communicating with others, there's no arrogance in what we say or in the tone that we use. Positive communicators care more about others than themselves, always in the good mood, or the right state of mind to listen and communicate with others. No negative communicator is pleasant to have a conversation with. Their conversation is always filled with negativity and harsh words, ready to hurt somebody's feelings.

Trust me on this one, negative communicators are not good listeners and always ready to interrupt others during conversation. Unfortunately, many brothers and sisters are not aware of just how often they use negative forms of communication to one another. When we act in such negative way toward each other, we are planting the seed of pain and suffering in the yard of each other. My question to you is this, is it really worth it? No, I don't think it's worth it to be the cause of your brothers' and sisters' pain and suffering. We have to learn how to talk to each other in a respectful and positive manner for less pain and suffering. Effective communication takes a lot of time and hard work. As we all know, nobody is perfect. We all make mistakes, but at the same time, there's a minimum that we can bring to the table. What's important is that each of us, as a human, should make the effort to communicate with compassion, understanding, and respect to one another. And as a result of such positive behavior would be a much better society and better relationship among people around the world.

If someone is not in the mood and finds himself or herself in a negative state of mind and can't be reason at present, please take a seat or walk out so you can limit your time spent trying to talk or help that person. Trust me, it will be a waste of your time trying to calm down or talk some sense out of an angry mind. If you really want to help that individual, do it at distance by trying to smooth talk him or her or just leave and come back later. Sincerely, you don't want to play with an angry dog. Understand that when you are a negative person, you only concentrate or focus on negative and bad things and can only see the full glass half full, "without judging anybody." And these kinds of people can only see the small picture, not the bigger. A negative person is very sensitive. He or she hates criticism. The bad part is, you can even say nice or kind things about a negative person and still take it the wrong way. It's a nightmare when you find yourself swimming in the deep pool of negativity, very deadly. It doesn't matter if you are a good swimmer or not. Trust me, you will drown. Most likely, they will also consider a funny joke like being disrespectful or rude to them. They take every little thing seriously or too seriously. In other words, they take everything personal. The way that we talk and act make others see who we really are. "It shows our true color." It's very important that we surrender ourselves with positive friends and successful people for our own good and success, people we can communicate with and gain something useful or beneficial to us. When we're trying to communicate with one another, and we have a feeling that the conversation might take another level, a negative one, try our best to stay calm and positive because some people can be very annoying and disrespectful. When we are having a discussion with somebody and you have a feeling that things might get heated, as a positive person, listen with compassion and understanding by listening more with open ears and keep silence.

By doing so, you simply throw water on the fire than gasoline. Such strategy will bring back effective communication to the discussion. Also when having an argument, don't focus on the negative side of it; see the positive side only, the other side of communication.

Some conversations can be very frustrating and irritating. Still do your best to keep it positive. Negative people let their anger or temper control their lives and attitudes, and that's a very ugly and dangerous situation. No matter how angry we are as human beings, we must still be able to control our temper. If you can't do that simple task, you will end up doing or saying regretful things. Please don't let this happen to you; it's like putting your two feet in one shoe. My best advice to you is when you find yourselves in such predicament, heated situation, the best and smart thing to do is walk away before it gets out of hand. Use compassion and understanding while keeping your cool and positivity in order to deactivate tension. Remember, "Vautoir's antidote" will always be helpful. When you walk away, it doesn't mean that you are a coward or a chicken, it simply says that you are a very smart person. In the negative person's mind-set, he or she can only see you as a coward or a chicken. It's okay, let them call you or picture you as a coward or chicken; understand this, they have no understanding whatsoever of anything. There's a say in Creole, which is my beautiful language: "A coward will bury his father and mother, but a brave man will find himself dead or behind bars." By acting so smart, you avoid drama and conflicts, even save lives before anyone can even realize what you are doing so cleverly. That's being positive and smart. That's turning negative into positive by manipulating the negativity in a good way. Such tactic will also help keep the peace and manage properly your relationships between husband and wife, romantic partners, coworkers, friends, and family members, etc. It's a great feeling when you feel like everything is going to be all right. It's a great accomplishment also when you can slide away from tense situations, you just turn yourself into a hero by visiting "the other side of communication" and keep communication alive. If there is no positive thing to say in a discussion, it's better to keep quiet than saying negative or hurtful things that can make the other person suffer. Some harsh words are more hurtful and dangerous than regular weapons; therefore, let us be "mindful" when communicating with others. When you sense that a conversation is about to go down the hill, try to change the subject real quick, like pulling the hand break of a vehicle with no breaks at all. As they say, "Better to be safe than sorry." It's in anybody's best interest to walk away in a middle of an argument or discussion no matter where it may take place. Then you will realize that the power is in your hand to flip things over and keep the peace and everyone safe. As positive people, it's our duty to try our best to approach others in a respectful manner so we can receive the positive feedback that we deserve.

Mindful Awareness

When you communicate in a mindful way, compassion and positivity put you behind a bulletproof glass where you don't have to worry about any bullets because you are well protected, and people around you will have least to worry about. They feel as though if you are protected, they are also protected (self-secured). By listening and watching those around you, you will see the result of your compassion and positivism that you produce among them by the way they communicate and respond to you. That is also a form of reproduction. That is exactly why you shouldn't talk and listen to any negative person. They can put your health at risk. Without mindfulness of awareness, you become a hazardous material to yourself and other people simply because you don't think before you talk and act; therefore, you become unaware of those awesome things on the other side of communication. A positive mind-set, mindful conversation and communication is a juicy fruit that we can devour together that we will find only on the other side of communication. Positive communication brings compassion, understanding, care, love, and peace of mind to others.

There is nothing better than having a positive conversation. From experience, I can say that we're still little babies who need to learn how to crawl, walk, and learn how to talk when it comes to communication. Why? Well, we are still learning how to communicate with ourselves and others in a positive way. Most of us, as human beings, have no clue of what is going on within us. In a sense, we are really disconnected with life and ourselves. We are talking while we think that we are sleeping. We are walking and we think that we are running. We sit at a table eating. We think we are somewhere out there dancing; therefore, we are lost and confused. We do need to communicate more with anyone, strangers included. Communication is the only route that will drop us where we need to be so we can find ourselves and think clearly. Talking or communicating with ourselves and others in a positive way is a revolutionary act. It is what it is because you move from one state of mind to another, meaning you broke the silence cycle. That is exactly what I call the other side of communication, period. Let us start nourishing ourselves by reading, writing, and communicating in a positive manner from now on. Let us say, for instance, we decide to write a letter to whomever, and such letter is written with understanding and compassion. Know that you are not nourishing only that person you are sending that precious letter to, but you also nourishing yourself as the writer of such letter. Dear brothers and sisters, make sure your writing, e-mails, texts, or while talks on the phone you use mindfulness and positive communication that will be very healthy for you and the person that you are talking or writing to. By doing so, you will avoid to break somebody's heart or feelings to push someone to committing suicide and make him feel less than a person.

Next time you are writing, e-mailing someone, or using your phone to talk to somebody, make sure you use positive communication or mindful communication. The real purpose of such attitude is to help people to communicate with respect, understanding, and compassion, at the same time save lives. As human beings, we just turn it around like we turn everything else around or upside down to our own benefit or advantage even though it will make others suffer or destroy the world, "who cares right!" Remember, if you use respect, understanding, and compassion when you are talking with someone, it can be in person or over the phone, I guarantee you 100 percent that this same individual will talk to you in the same manner. It doesn't matter if he is a respectful and compassionate person or not, you will rip what you sow or you will eat what you bring to the table, and there is no doubt about it. Therefore, if you pick up a phone to call a friend, a family member, your job, or whatever the case may be, talk with respect, understanding, and compassion. It applies also when you are talking with someone one on one. Together we can spread positive communication around the world that will affect everyone like a terrible disease that comes with no antidote. We can change this world by the way we communicate and treat each other. I am so comfortable in thinking and talking positively I feel as though there is no other way to express myself.

Effective Communication

Effective communication is way deeper than just changing ideas, words, and information. It allows you to communicate better while avoiding misunderstandings and improve yourself in every area of communication. You will also have the ability to comprehend the emotion and intentions behind the information given. Know that effective communication doesn't come by without a good listening skill. With both skills combined (effective communication and good listening skills), you will have the power to convey any message given or talking to groups because you will have a better understanding of what you have told and spoken about. And for some of us, someone will tell us something or just have a nice conversation with us and think we understood and heard everything clearly, but we were mistaken. We had a misunderstanding of everything that was said and heard when it's time to talk about it or explain it to somebody else or a group, you find yourself confused because it creates a lot of confusion and frustration within you (awkward situation), not only to you but to the people or group that you are trying to explain what you have been taught or learned. That is why it is a must for us to work on our communication and listening skills so we can avoid such embarrassment. Whether we are trying to improve our communication so we can talk or communicate effectively to groups, to our peers, to our spouse, or to build greater trust or whatever the case may be, those two skills will rise up your confidence and will deepen your connections to other people (communication and listening skills). They are twins. They cannot live without one another. If you try to separate them and think that you can do okay by doing so, you're just lying and confusing yourselves, and that is a fact. You cannot have an effective communication or talk effectively if you do not know how to listen.

If you want to speak effectively, you have to be able to twist or flip what you are saying or the communication that you are having or about to have by simply looking for the other side of communication. You may ask yourself, how am I going to do that? Well, my answer to you would be you just have to know way much more than what you are going to talk about. In order to do that, you will need these six amazing components. It's that simple.

- Always focus on the person or audience that you are addressing.
- Make sure that you engage a conversation with them so they can feel part of what's going on (communicate with passion).
- Know how to articulate (think before you talk), and let the truth be told.

- Your opinion has to be very powerful. Whatever you are trying to pass on or express, make it worthwhile of your audience or the person that you are trying to convince.
- Show emotion in what you are saying. By convincing yourself, then only then you will be able to convince other people.
- Raise the bar. Make the audience believe if this doesn't happen, this can be the end of the world or something terrible will happen to our nation (make them believe).

There are two forms of communications: consumption and nourishment.

Consumption. In the category of consumption, I found the internet that is full of good and bad, toxic or healing for the mind body and soul. From my point of view, the internet has more toxins than healing. It doesn't mean that you have to stay away from the internet. You just have to be careful of what you are reading, writing, and watching. When you spend a lot of time on the computer watching toxic things, know that you are lost. It's like you are driving to a location for the first time with no GPS, imagine that. We got to be aware of what we are consuming because what we read, what we write about, and whom we choose to be with can damage us for the rest of our lives, even poison our brain. Reading, writing, and choosing to be with positive people can nourish your minds and bodies; therefore, be aware of what you consume (mindfulness).

Nourishment. No one can survive without food. It is impossible. Everything that we eat as human beings has an effect on us (good or bad), either to poison us and kill us or to heal us. We, as individuals, have a tendency to think nourishment is only what we put in our mouths and swallow without knowing what we listen to, what we write about, what we watch, whom we talk to, and what we talk about is also food that nourish our bodies, minds, and souls. Simple things like that, you know everybody would know, not really.

The kind of conversations that we are listening to or taking part of is also food. My question to my readers is, are you cooking and eating the quality food that will keep you healthy mentally and physically? What we should know as humans is that when we say or engage a positive or effective communication, we nourish ourselves and uplift people around us and grow. By having such positive attitude, we're just feeding love and compassion to those around us, and that's good seed.

Self-Taught

Taking a deep breath, or inhaling and exhaling, is a method that teaches us how to keep quiet and listen to ourselves. By using such discipline, we will, by benefit, improve our communication. Please try to do this as often as possible (breathe in, breathe out). Such method will prove to us that if we are able to listen and communicate with ourselves, then for sure we will do so with others. It is impossible to communicate with other people if we can't communicate with ourselves. That is the truth. Learning to keep quiet and listening to ourselves is imperative to a good communicator. And by holding hands with such formula, it will help us cross the bridge of communication so we can see its other side. By being silent and listening, we are communicating with ourselves by bringing the mind and the body together on the door steps of breathing in and breathing out. That is healthy communication within us. Isn't that the other side of communication? When we inhale and exhale (deep breathing), there is a connection between our body and mind. This is a breathing method, also called diaphragmatic breathing, and that is giving full oxygen to the body. I have learned from my research that deep breathing is more efficient. It allows our body to fully exchange in coming oxygen with outgoing carbon dioxide. They have also been shown to slow the heartbeat, lower or stabilize blood pressure, and lower stress. If anybody really want to experience deep breathing, it is recommended to find a comfortable and quiet place to sit or lie down.

  Start developing the habit of thinking and talking positively to yourself and others, it will be very helpful down the line or in the future. Anybody who can develop such a skill will have the ability to communicate positively. Learning to communicate with yourself is teaching yourself how to communicate with ease. And you will also learn how to communicate effectively and clearly in every situation. Many of us don't know that we can also communicate with ourselves, even teach ourselves. Communication doesn't mean two people talking or having a conversation. It is deeper than that because we can also communicate with ourselves. We call it self-communication; it's the things we think about, things we say to ourselves, and the way we let others treat us or talk to us; that is what we get used to and runs through our minds. Therefore, our thoughts, our attitudes and behaviors are very important communicators to ourselves but ourselves. You see, brothers and sisters, developing a positive way to communicate with yourselves is an imperative to keep you healthy and happy. Such attitude will show you and prove to others that you are someone that values and honors your life (intrapersonal communication), meaning to communicate with one's self. It's awesome to talk to yourself as a person, especially asking yourself valuable questions. There is absolutely nothing wrong with that. And trust me, you are not crazy. You're just enriching your brain. Let me ask you this, do you really want to know and to become a real professional in self-taught or self-communication? Well, if you do, do what I did; talk to a mirror. It can be the one in your room, living room, or bathroom, it really doesn't matter. Talk to yourself in that mirror and consider your reflection your best friend, a family member, or a stranger, whatever you feel comfortable of, making it even though in your subconscious. You already know it's just a reflection of you, but try not to see it that way. See the other side or the other level of it that will take you to the journey of self-taught. When you communicate or have a conversation with a mirror, if your name is Jean, say, for example, "Jean, you can do this." And the minute you're done saying it, take a deep breath (breathe in and breathe out). It will help you think deeper and clearly, which researchers have proven to be true. Research has also proven people who use their own name rather than "I" when engaging appositive self-talk are actually more supportive and encouraging to themselves. As people, we communicate with ourselves, every second, every minute every hour, every day, every week, every year; unfortunately, not everybody knows that. Self-communication determines our lives, our quality, our self-respect, and our choices in life. Not many people understand that whatever we do in life is a choice. It is a choice because that's what we have decided to do. We choose to go down that path; therefore, whatever the outcome may be (good or bad). It's a choice that we have to deal with.

It takes me fifty years to understand and grab real hard on this concept and never let go to a point where it has turn me into a new man. When we practice self-communication, we're just putting oil in our three engines which are emotions, high self-esteem, and self-confidence.

Emotions: From what I have learned, emotion is a natural instinctive state of mind deriving from one's circumstances, mood or instinct/intuition, relationships with others, feelings, sentiment, and sensations. Most of us as humans understand that no engine can run without the proper oil. It doesn't matter what brand it is. As people, we are very emotional, and that's what get us in trouble easily. As human beings, our emotions control our thoughts, behaviors, attitudes, and actions. Brothers and sisters, if we have the ability to master our emotions, it would be very easy to master all of the above. And that is the best way to master ourselves—communication skills which is also a self-talk to ourselves in our own mind.

High self-esteem: In psychology, the term *self-esteem* is used to describe a person's overall sense of self-worth or personal value, in other words, how much you appreciate and like yourself. Self-esteem is often seen as a personality trait, which means that it tends to be stable and enduring. I want you to know, according to my research, self-esteem is extremely important because it heavily influences people's choices and decisions—meaning, self-esteem serves a motivational function by making it more or less likely that people will take care of themselves and explore their full potential. Self-esteem refers to a person's beliefs about his/her own work value. Those with high self-esteem are people who believe they can achieve anything in life, people who know how to take good care of themselves and who knows how to communicate with themselves and who expect to go very far in life to embrace their dreams. When it comes to people with low self-esteem, it's the opposite. They don't believe in themselves. They don't think that they can accomplish anything in life. They don't communicate with themselves in a positive way, and they are not persistent. They scared of failure, of criticism, and very resilient in terms of overcoming adversity. I want each and every one of you to understand something; when a person thinks that he is not worthy, that's considered also as low self-esteem. It's not okay, and it will never be okay to have low self-esteem.

Self-confidence: "Self-confidence is a feeling of trust in one's abilities, qualities, and judgement. To be self-confident, is to be secure in yourself and your abilities. When you are giving a presentation or a speech, it helps to be self-confident or at least to pretend that you are. Confidence is a feeling of trust in someone or something." Self-confidence is a must, it's one's ability to judge his own social and personal standing with respect to his environment and be able to derive satisfaction out of it. Self-confidence is influenced by factors like upbringing, work environment, and levels of dedication toward pursuing a cause or a dream. So self-communication has many branches as you can see. When you are talking and asking yourself some important questions, you are not only putting yourself in a mindful awareness, just to talking and acting positively, but you are also helping yourself to achieve great things (success). You are helping yourself also to walk all over self-doubts and self-induced fear. Please be kind to yourself so you can be kind to others. Talk to yourself with respect, understanding, and compassion; and by doing so, you will treat other people just like you treat yourselves.

Believe it or not, the quality of communication that we use to talk to others affect them in a good way or a bad way. That's exactly why God says, "Treat others the way you want to be treated," which unfortunately most of us took for granted. When you say to yourself, "I don't care about life or my surroundings," "I am nobody, and I hate myself," what do you think such negative thinking do to you and other people around you? If you don't care about your own life, what makes you think that you are going to care about other people's lives? If you don't believe in yourself, how can you believe in other people? If you hate yourself so much, what makes you think that you are capable to love others? It's a "must" to think positively and to stay in the mode of mindful awareness. People who think in such manner (negative way) are full of guilt, sadness, regrets, anger, suicidal thoughts, or tendencies. Negative thinking brings negative actions and affects the way we see ourselves, others, and the world; therefore, it will affect the quality of our lives. Life is not that complicated, brothers and sisters. Let us make the best out of it! Every day that the Lord gives you permission to wake up, thank him for it, and try your best to make that day worthy for you and others. Inspire yourself and others. Stimulate innovation, compassion, love, and encouragement. You think and talk in a positive way to yourself. Certainly you are going to have positive results because it's going to affect your life in a positive way, and it's that simple. When you are part in a society that gives you a nationality, know that you have a part of responsibility through this nation. In order to know what your part of responsibility is, first you have to hunt down your destiny. Finding your destiny is finding the light that will guide you on your path to your goal in life. Trust me, your goal is going to be useful to you and the society that you are living in. That is part of your responsibility that you will put in action. This is a very serious matter. It's something that you cannot take lightly. Always find a way to better yourself and the society that you are part of, and such attitude or way of thinking will raise your personal bar of excellence. And acting so, you can live a healthy life.

You will positively affect your nation and people around you, just like an electric shock of a high voltage because other people will take notice and will improve themselves by letting their light shine just like yours. You will create a mind-set or be mindful of people that think of others before themselves, something that greedy people in this world that we are living in need to understand. It's a mindful of compassion, understanding, innovation, dignity, integrity, and ingenuity. Either way, you look at such a collective mind-set of brothers and sisters would do great to your nation and would become the foundation of this wonderful nation. In this case, you are the driver of the bus. It starts with you and only you.

Consequences of Miscommunication

Scientists believe, humans began speaking about one hundred thousand years ago, and writing began around 4000 BC. Prior to written languages, humans used pictures (cave drawings), which evolved to word symbols (the evolution of language, what some have called the human system of communication). What we need to know is that communication is not one way street; otherwise, it wouldn't be named *communication*. It's a two-way street. Communication comes about one person who wants to convey to another person (one talk, the other listen). The one listening is the one receiving the message that the other person wants to pass on. Know that the message that the talker brings can also be misunderstood. Communication is the blood that gives life to any relationship, organization, politician, and marriage, etc. Imagine for one second living our lives without any communication whatsoever. It's like not having any blood running through our vein at all; that would be a disaster, wouldn't it?

We have the responsibility to communicate clearly to one another if we really want to understand each other. The absence of good communication can breed confusion, frustration, division, and lack of understanding, etc. Please let us talk in a clear manner when to communicate to one another. It's imperative to a good communicator.

Alvernia University said that each and every human being has his or her way or style to communicate or interact and exchange information with others. They are four basic of communication styles: passive, aggressive, passive-aggressive, and assertive. It is important to understand each communication style and why individuals use them. For example, the assertive communication style has been found to be most effective because it incorporates the best aspects of all the other styles.

When we break down these four styles, we'll better understand the characteristics of each style, standards, phrases, and what make them unique.

Passive

Individuals who use the passive communication style often act indifferently, yielding to others. Passive communicators usually fail to express their feelings or needs, allowing others to express themselves. Frequently, a passive communicator's lack of outward communication can lead to misunderstanding, anger build-up, or resentment. At the same time, these communicators can be safer to speak with when a conflict arises because they most likely will avoid a confrontation or defer to others.

Passive communicators always display a lack of eye contact, poor body posture, and an inability to say no. Passive communicators also act in a way that states "people never consider my feelings." But passive communicators are also easy to get along with as they follow others and "go with the flow."

Example of phrases that those who use a passive communication style would say or may believe include the followings:

* "It really doesn't matter that much."
* "I just want to keep the peace."

Aggressive communicators

It's often apparent when someone communicates in an aggressive manner. You'll hear it. You'll see it. You may even feel it.

The aggressive communication style is emphasized by speaking in a loud and demanding voice, maintaining intense eye contact and dominating or controlling others by blaming, intimidating, criticizing, threatening, or attacking them, among other traits. Aggressive communicators often issue commands, ask questions rudely, and fail to listen to others. But they can also be considered leaders and command respect from those around them.

Examples of phrases that an aggressive communicator would use include the followings:

- "I'm right, and you're wrong."
- "I'll get my way no matter what."
- "It's all your fault."

Passive-aggressive

Passive-aggressive communication style users appear passive on the surface; but within, he or she may feel powerless or stuck, building up a resentment that leads to seeing things or acting out in subtle, indirect, or secret ways. Most passive-aggressive communicators will mutter to themselves rather than confront a person or issue. They have difficulty acknowledging their anger, use facial expressions that don't correlate with how they feel, and even deny there is a problem. Passive-aggressive communicators are most likely to communicate with body language or a lack of open communication to another person, such as giving someone the silent treatment, speaking rumors behind people's backs, or sabotaging others' efforts. Passive-aggressive communicators may also appear cooperative but may silently do the opposite.

Ultimately, passive-aggressive communicators are aware of their needs but at times struggle to voice them.

Examples of phrases that a passive-aggressive communicator would use include the followings:

- "That's fine with me, but don't be surprised if someone else gets mad."
- "Sure, we can do things your way," then mutters to self that "your way is stupid.

Assertive communicators

Thought to be the most effective form of communication, the assertive communication style features an open communication link while not being over bearing. Assertive communicators can express their own needs, desires, ideas, and feelings while also considering the needs of others. Assertive communicators aim for both sides to win in a situation, balancing one's rights with the rights of others.

One of the keys of assertive communication is using "I" statements, such as "I feel frustrated when you are late for a meeting," or, "I don't like having to explain this over and over." It indicates ownership of feelings and behaviors without blaming the other person.

Examples of phrases an assertive communicator would use include the followings:

- "We are equally entitled to express ourselves respectfully to one another."
- "I realize I have choices in my life, and I consider my opinions."
- "I respect the rights of others."

How to Become an Assertive Communicator

Understanding how others communicate can be key to getting your message across to them. In order to develop a more assertive communication style, here are a few tips to keep in mind:

- Take ownership (use "I" statements).
- Maintain eye contact.
- Learn to say "no."
- Voice your needs and desire confidently.

THE OTHER SIDE OF COMMUNICATION

Deep listening

    Deep listening is an awesome practice. If anybody that is listening could listen with compassion and understanding, they would be able to help others and help themselves by believing that they are not alone. In order to be able to listen to others, learn to listen to yourselves first. Deep listening is also about meditation, the reunion of the mind and the body for a better result. It's always in anybody's interest to communicate better or become a good communicator. When someone listens and speaks carefully, honestly, and compassionately, this person becomes automatically a better speaker, listener, and communicator because such individual crosses the barrier of diversity to lay the egg of deep listening. Brothers and sisters, the tree of deep listening can grow some juicy fruits like joy, happiness, love, understanding, compassion, wisdom, and caring by helping others carry their grief or burden. It shows that deep listening is an awesome practice that can help people grow and move forward. If you don't practice mindfulness and understanding, you will not care of others, and you will not take any interest in listening to their difficulties and problems. When you listen to the speaker or the person talking with awareness and understanding, you just bring your support to that human being so he can see and understand things differently or have another perspective of things. Let us say, for example, the person you are listening to is in the state of mind to commit suicide and full of anger, hate, and bitterness. Don't you know listening deeply and showing understanding to that particular person can change his negative feelings and thoughts to positive and change his life and mind forever? Therefore, understanding, compassion, and awareness should be present in our conversation and communication. That's what we should practice at all times. I guarantee to anybody as human beings, if we could let the seed of our understanding grow and water the seed of our mindfulness/awareness, it would, without a doubt, kill the seed of anger and false judgement in our hearts.

    It's impossible to be able to listen to others without listening to ourselves first. If you believe that your quality of listening is bad, all you got to do is train yourselves to inhale and exhale while focusing in what you need to listen to. Know how to listen is crucial, but going to deep listening is something else. It's another level of doing things the way we should. It's all about concentration and meditation, "mindful breathing." When we are listening to others, make sure that we listen with understanding while we are making sure that we do take them out of their worry zone and place them in a more relax and comfortable area where they feel safe. Whenever you have the chance to listen to someone, listen with one purpose and one purpose only—to let that person know that you care.

Keep the awareness of deep listening in your mind and heart so you can make this important phone call to compassion even though what the other person is talking about is full of wrong perceptions, hate, anger, accusations, and misunderstanding; I want you to know that you are safe simply because you are on the corner of compassion. Know when to focus on your listening, when to talk or give advice so that person can correct his perceptions and misunderstanding. When you turn and keep the switch of compassion on, you don't have anything to worry about. Compassion is present; you are protected because you will be able to listen mindfully. And the person that you are listening to will be able to determine if you're really listening with care and understanding. The minute that person touches the ground of comfort, he will keep talking without stopping, thanks to your compassion toward him/her. When you don't care about yourself, you won't care about others. In that case, you make yourself and others suffer. But if you listen deeply to what they have to say and you believe what they are saying come from suffering, be aware that they are protected by your compassion. Show them that you are here for them and you care. In that case, you cannot judge them nor blame them because of the trust that they place in you. By listening deeply and compassionately to the other person, you begin to understand that person better and love grows. Love is not possible without the presence of understanding; it gives birth to love. Every human being on earth is hungry for love. If you really love someone and you want to make that person happy, you just have to show some understanding, appreciation, and gratitude.

THE OTHER SIDE OF COMMUNICATION

Without these three elements, there is no happiness. Showing someone that you care by listening deeply with compassion is an essential ingredient for generating understanding so deep inside of you can rest true love. If understanding is the mother of love, then you can also say that love is the foundation of understanding. Remember, in my deep thinking, I said understanding gave birth to love, and love gave birth to happiness. Therefore, there is no happiness without love and understanding. You see it's a family thing. As humans, we have a lack of understanding and love, and that's exactly why we don't care about one another the way we should. Love, understanding, and happiness are triplets. How can anybody care for anybody else without this beautiful package? How can parents really love their children without showing that they understand and care for them? Many people don't engage conversation or communicate to others simply by thinking that they will be misunderstood. Nobody wants to be misunderstood. It's a terrible feeling, trust me. That is why so many people are reluctant to start a conversation or communicate with others.

However, their doors are wide open to welcome anyone who would like to step in and start a conversation with them. Such speaker or communicator has to use compassion and understanding so the addressee can feel secure and cared for. Also, the communicator or the starter has to make sure that he goes to deep listening so when the listener starts speaking that he speaks, avoiding all doubts that he may have and think that he is getting all the attention that he deserves or wants. Sure enough, this person will tell you about his difficulties with no hesitation. You can even ask him, do you think that I have listened to you with compassion enough? Trust and believe, he will tell you exactly how he feels, and that's what I call "the language of understanding." Such language does not apply without deep listening that will take you straight to the mood of "mindful awareness."

When we listen deeply with compassion to our romantic partner, friend, family member, group, husband, or wife, know that we will benefit as well. It will place us right in the mode called "peace of mind" because it will help us to see and understand things that we wouldn't be able to see and understand when we were full of judgement, anger, resentment, blame, and hate. Listening with compassion brings peaceful and happy living. Listening deeply to others is putting compassion in the boiled pot of understanding for a delicious communication so together we can sit at a dinner table and enjoy this delicious meal. Deep listening is the best way to learn. In order to get into the zone of deep listening, it requires for the moment a red card to wrong perceptions and a willingness to open our door to welcome new information whether they are negative, positive, or else. When we are listening deeply to someone, make sure that we don't only listen to the words of the speaker but to the speaker in whole, his moves. The way he moves is a form of speaking also, and that's when we listen to the entire speaker in whole. When we go about, we will hear every dimension of the speaker, both of what he is talking about, as well as what he is implying. With such technique, we will be able to hear the words, the phrases, the gestures, and the emotions hiding underneath them and able to see what kind of state of mind "mood" that the speaker find himself in.

The Power of Deep Listening

Listening deeply is very powerful. Listening" to a speaker is one thing, but understanding what he tries to pass on is quite another. We can listen to so many speakers in our lifetime and still don't get anything from what they have talked about. It is a waste of time if we don't know how to listen deeply, and that's where the power of an effective communicator lies.

Communicating is not about what we say or the kind of conversation that we are having, rather what our listeners hear and understand. Such branch is attaches to all relationships, romantic relationship, friendship, etc. A person that you are talking to can hear you talking and can even hear everything that you talked about and still don't understand because he didn't really listen to you "deep listening." Guest what, this is the nightmare of all relationships and marriages.

"The psychology of hearing teaches us that hearing involves sound waves, eardrums, the cochlea and thousands of tiny hair cells that turn vibrations into electrical signals. These signals tell the brain you are hearing a noise, and identify what the noise is."

Practical and Listening Strategy

I've learned that hearing is the practical, and listening is the strategy. Practical is a method likely to succeed or to be effective in real circumstances; empirical strategy is a plan of action or policy designed to achieve a major or overall aim said *Oxford*.

A good communicator knows exactly the type of listening skills to use in every situation and how to use them to his listeners' advantage.

Here are four strategies to many types of listening that are the followings:

- Listening awareness

    When using awareness, you will listen effectively. Such strategy can help any type of relationship and brings solution to the barriers of miscommunication, anger, accusation, hate, wrong perception, and frustration, meaning that it can help us to communicate better and also help us understand better. It surely can expand both our understanding and communication, in a society, in relationships, etc. It brings to the table efficiency and productivity.
- Mindful listening

    Mindful listening is listening to a speaker without interference by letting that person express himself without cutting him off. This is reaching for effective communication, healthy listening, good understanding, and connection. I truly believe that every communicator should take a dose of Vautoir's antidote so they can be in the right mood when it comes to communication.

- Passionate listening

    The same level of passion that you use as a speaker is required also as a listener. Whenever you have the chance to listen to somebody or a group, please listen with passion. Communication is only effective when both of you know when to listen and when to talk. Do me a big favor; use passion in your relationships and marriages so they can last. Do it for the children's sake.
- Active listening

    Active listening is the master key that opens the door of effective communication. It requires a lot of effort, and such strategy surpasses hearing. It is way above hearing. The fact of the matter is that you can hear someone without listening. We hear that often, don't we? "I hear you" or I hear that" is very common. Deep concentration will take you to meet with active listening so you can become best friends and forget about hearing. Therefore, "I hear you" will be no more.

Listen with Compassion

When we listen with compassion, we listen with real interest "compassionate listening." When we take a close look at compassion, what do we see? We see understanding, which means that compassion gives birth to understanding. It is our duty as human beings to understand the pain and suffering of each other and avoid to make one another suffer. It is imperative to take the time to listen with compassion and understanding to what others are saying, are going through. I beg you, please let us do our best to practice compassion and understanding. Most of us listen to others just to judge them or bad mouth them. Why not listen to the sufferer so we can bring healing? Listening with an open heart will allow the sufferer to be himself with no worries. That is compassion and understanding at their best, reaching to the sufferers so they can ease their doubts and worries. What a great feeling. Listening with compassion, opens the gate of communication to a deep mutual understanding.

By taking time to listen with compassion and understanding the pain and suffering of others, we can easily carry them to a whole different state of mind and make them believe that they are not alone and there are others that care about them. It is a total and complete healing, "Vautoir's antidote" for life.

Listening compassionately requires wisdom, love, positivity, openness, and a lot of understanding. It also requires *open mind*, so no judgement can go through while exercising or practicing these skills. It demands to listen carefully to the sufferer. *Listen with interest*, and that's exactly when our focus and concentration will rise and open our eyes for a better understanding. When the speaker or the sufferer is talking, make sure that we make eye contact because it will automatically reveal to the sufferer that you are listening with compassion, and you care. Why don't we let our heart guide us instead of our mind so we can really make a difference in other people's lives? Together we can leave something good and positive for generations to come.

Listening with compassion is not listen just to listen, but listening with open ears. When we listen with open ears, we listen more deeply and clearly. And when we listen more deeply and clearly, we knock on the door of compassion. And I can say this, brothers and sisters, when we are able to listen with compassion to what someone has to say or the suffering of others, we not only make that person or people feel secure, but also it shows them that others do care about them. Such behavior is not only beneficial to them only but to us as well. We will benefit because we will feel peaceful with ourselves, doing the right thing, "mindfulness." Listening with compassion is listening peacefully in a state of mind that will chase away all negativity, such as hate, anger, judgment, perception, etc. It will put us in a mood where happiness and understanding live. Compassion makes us see and understand things that we would be unable to see and understand when walking and embracing negative feelings. When we listen with open ears, we are not only listening with open ears but also with an open mind (mindfulness). When we listen deeply with open ears, in a heartbeat, compassion is born. And with that precious birth, we can have peace in our lives. Please listen with open ears so compassion can be within you. Even though we are sad or angry for whatever reason, our compassion will crush our sadness and anger and bring us the peace of mind that we deserve. The seed of fear, vengeance, and anger in each and every human being is a deadly weapon to humanity because of the way we think and act. Therefore, it's our duty as human beings to water the right seed which is compassion, love, and understanding for a better generation to come. Some brothers and sisters suffer a lot. Life becomes very dark for them, and all they can see is darkness. And that is why we should have great compassion for people like these. Some turn themselves into killers, and others turn to drugs and alcohol. It could have been me and you. That's why we should take them in consideration and have compassion for them. Whoever find themselves in such situation suffer a lot, and life becomes very dark.

Wrong perceptions are in every area in our lives, and as long they persist, the number of criminals and drug users will only increase, and it will always be difficult to control them in the society that we are part of. As long as those problems (poverty, criminality, drugs, and alcohol) exist, it's endless, and that's a fact. When we look deeply at the problem of the world is facing, we have to look at them with compassion and understanding. When we act in such a positive manner, others will watch and will listen. They will know what to do, what not to do, what to say and what not to say, what to consume and what not to consume, in order to discontinue this kind of pain and suffering they are going through. We need to learn how to address others with respect, compassion, and understanding so we don't increase or multiply the despair, the hate, and anger in people. Instead, why not turn ourselves into the right motivational speakers and explain to them why things are the way they are, why do they happen, and what can be done to reverse them so their compassion can rise and grow. As humans, we can make a huge difference with the practice of listening with open ears; therefore, the solution is not too far from us. Let us practice compassion and understanding together so we can get rid of the suffering of others and live our lives with a clear conscience. Peace be with us.

THE OTHER SIDE OF COMMUNICATION

Deep Thinking

The minute we start taking deep breaths, it means that we start listening to our senses that drive us directly to our thoughts mindfully with attention. Everyone on this planet earth has a sense of thinking. Some of us use it entirely, some a little bit, and others don't use it at all. Some of us think before we act. We think about the consequences before we say and do things. It means that we asked ourselves some valuable questions like "if I do this, what will be the result or the outcome? Can I say this the way I want to say it? Will it affect others?" For those who think a little bit have random thinking. The minute they think something, they say it without giving it a second thought, no questions asked, or they just think after the facts. For those who don't think at all will say anything full of toxic and don't care about the damage it causes. They don't even think after the facts, not at all. Brothers and sisters, be aware that when it comes to deep thinking, it's not as common as you think it is. Not everybody knows or can think deeply. Deep thinking can accommodate anybody's life, dreams, and communication. It means that if we think deeply the way we should, it can change or transform our lives. It can flip over the way we think and show us the other side of communication. It can transform our behaviors, attitudes, and feelings. There is no greater power than that, power of thinking and communicating.

The only lesson I got from all this is that it teaches me that the other side of communication is full of greatness. Deep thinking is very beneficiary to those who embrace it and will introduce it to positive communication. When thinking deeply, it simply means that we are capable of thinking beyond our understanding and beliefs while flipping over the table of communication just to show us the other side. Thinking deeply also means to crush down all false convictions so the truth can be told with no hesitation (shall be the light). The biggest problem that the world has to face right now is the way that we think. We, as human beings, we don't know how to think positively or the right way. Our thinking is not focused on the right things. It is not balance and directed or guided. It doesn't matter to a lot of us that thinking randomly is okay. It is also okay not to give our thinking much thought. Therefore, the way that we think weakens our process of thinking positively or deeply. So because of such weakness, we fail to think beyond our own boundaries. We fail to succeed. We fail to communicate the way we should, and we even fail to teach ourselves positive attitudes and behaviors; therefore, we fail ourselves and others that rely on us. Thinking deeply is a magnet that can change our lives and people around us. Start today introducing yourselves to deep thoughts, and you will see how your life will change for the better. And it can also change the world because the way we think can flip it over. What we believe in and the way we think can influence the way we feel and behave. "What you think you become." We have to have the ability to think vigorously. By thinking in such a manner, by thinking deeply is simply jumping to the other side of communication. We will be able to ease our way of communication, understanding, and compassion. It will turn on the light switch of our brain to a more inquisitive and reflective approach of thinking and acting. By knowing how to think deeply, we just dig deeper and deeper to create a solid foundation of communication and meaningful life to lie on. Deep thinking teaches us that there are other ways of thinking. We can think negatively and positively. We can have some imaginary ideas and some destructive ones without necessary or having an obligation to accept them. By thinking deeply, we have a better chance to think positively and come up with some thoughts that are more valuable and meaningful to us and our surroundings. When we behave in such way, it greatly influences our attitudes and actions. It even influences the way we talk to people and ease our communication. Therefore, we can see that deep thinking really have the power to upgrade our actions, attitudes, behaviors, and communication to a more meaningful valuable existence as humans. My questions to you today are the followings: Are you satisfied with your way of thinking? Do you like the outcome? The way we think can be healthy or unhealthy. Positive thoughts create supportive beliefs, which can support us through our difficult times. At the other end, negative thoughts will force us or dictate us to give up when things are tough and unbearable. Don't you think that it is time for a change?

It is time for us to start turning things around so we can begin pulling deep thinking into our lives! Thinking and talking to ourselves is an awesome way we can start searching for the other side of communication. Either way, we win, can't lose.

The method we should use to think deeply is divided into three sections:

- When you really want to think deep, make sure that you go someplace quiet in order to kick out of the curve all form of destruction that will stop you from concentrating.
- Make sure that you focus on what you are doing so nothing in the whole world can disturb you. Your attention is required to yourself and yourself only.
- Remember the higher quality thoughts that you dive into, the better (positive thinking).

The reason why I recommend to practice such method is because even though we might live in a noisy neighborhood, we can still think deeply when we all know that it is almost impossible to promote deep thinking in a noisy environment. But we still can do it with great concentration, plus "where there is a will, there is a way." Certainly it would be way much better for any of us to find a peaceful location where there is no noise or distractions at all. Such location will free our thoughts so our mind can land quietly. If we really want to go in such mood in our room, make sure that we buy a "do not disturb" sign to put on our doors so nobody disturbs us.

Distraction is a very bad thing when it comes to meditation and deep thinking. It will take us out of our way or out of our comfort zone of concentrating on positive thoughts. Noise and disturbance will keep us at the bottom to assure that we do not reach a deeper level of thinking and communicating. So it is more than a must or required to stay in the quietest environment in order to reduce the noise and distraction that can mess up our concentration. The nickname that I give to such tranquility is quietness for deeper thinking. It only happens when we turn off the TV, the CD player or radio, and throw away our cell phones (you know what I mean)! Do whatever it takes to be in a very quiet place when you are going to deep thinking. It's the law. Destruction from friends, neighbors, family members, or noise objects of the house, or wherever you might be, can sink our deep-thinking process that was floating on the surface level and prevent us from reaching our mindful awareness. Remember anything that is contrary of thinking is a threat to positive and deep thinking. If there is anything that can't encourage thinking, there is a possibility that this thing can become a destruction.

It is obvious that concentration is the best way to meet with deep thinking. If you can't concentrate, you will lose focus for sure. Concentration is the only element that can help us take a grab on our focus without letting unnecessary noises to interfere. However, it is not easy to concentrate, but with determination, everything is possible. Each and every one of us has to have the ability to learn and concentrate when we are thinking deeply. It is fundamental. To develop concentration in order to communicate well and think deep, some effort, dedication, and practice are recommended. Remember that saying, "Practice makes perfect." Our level of concentration can rise and shine. We just need to make the necessary efforts. That's what I call finding qualitative food for our thoughts, minds, bodies, and souls. That's a very healthy discovery. The other side of communication is full of knowledge and fun that will take you to meet with your destiny.

Nowadays, random thinking leaves its shadow behind and make it almost impossible and hard for quality and positive thinking to land. We feel so comfortable when it comes to superficial thinking. We even promote it to our children and the society that we are living in, what a mess! After giving it a deep thought, I asked myself three important questions:

- What happened to vigorous thinking?
- Where did it go?
- What are we doing to the children?

Can somebody please help me find these answers! I really believe that we are living in a shadow that is erasing gradually or fading away our senses to the point where we give up on the most important things in life. What I want you to understand, brothers and sisters, is that the way we think has a great effect on our lives, and it can transform it for the better or for the worse. It's up to us. Deep thinking leads to great and positive communication. It is impossible to communicate effectively without quality thoughts in your deep thinking. Know that irrelevant thoughts will take you nowhere; they have the power just like crack cocaine to damage your brain cells with no questions asked. Therefore, we don't need them, so stay away from them. The best way to work on your deep thinking is through books (reading). Reading is the best source of inspiration there is. It can really trigger the passion to think deeper.

Deep Understanding

For me, deep understanding is a puzzle that each and every human being should work hard to put together piece by piece, and use this puzzle or understanding to other people's advantage by solving problems, helping those in needs and search for new ideas.

Deep understanding is the whole package of knowledge, and those who are really striving for it always end up getting it so they can devour it with appetite. Knowledge is above everything. We use it to do everything such as playing an instrument, driving a car, a bus, a truck, writing a book, crossing a street, being a doctor, a nurse, an engineer, a carpenter, a mechanic, or a shoemaker, etc. Therefore, we can say that knowledge is very huge and has many branches just like a tree. And let me ask you this, where do you think knowledge comes from? It comes from deep understanding that give us the ability to do great things.

Understanding is about facts and principles so we can be familiar with or to be aware of "familiarity awareness." Understanding is a concept that requires a comprehensive grip of what we have learned or taught. In order to understand something, it requires a certain aspect of intelligence—comprehensive understanding. Sometimes we don't even have an explanation for what we think we understand. If we want a true and deep understanding, it requires more effort.

Let us say for example that we are readers, we read books; but unfortunately, the books that we read, we don't learn or apply anything good in our daily lives; no knowledge acquire "shallow understanding." But when we read positive books or motivational books and we apply almost everything that we have read in our daily lives, not only we acquire knowledge, but also we aim for success and a better life, deep understanding. That is commitment and engagement that will lift us and drop us off gently to the door steps of change.

"Shallow understanding" is just having the basic knowledge and understanding of something. It's the opposite of deep understanding. Our king used to talk about it, shallow understanding, who is, of course, our hero, Dr. Martin Luther King Jr. May he rest in peace.

Miscommunication

Miscommunication means to fail to communicate the way we should. Instead, we communicate to each other in a way to create confusion. Miscommunication is a killer, and that is exactly why communication around the world find itself lying on its back on a hospital bed in a deep coma. It is not wise to keep communicating with our friends, family members, romantic partners, etc., inadequately, unclearly, and mistakenly. When we communicate to one another, we pass information to each other. Now it's how we want to convey such information. It can be person to person, writing, texting, concepts, ideas, thoughts. Emotions are exchanged. With regrets, miscommunication is more common than we think.

Most readers and listeners fail to understand what they have read or listened to. Miscommunication represents a nightmare around the world to church leaders, teachers, industrials, politicians, big corporations, management, families, friendships, romantic relationships, nations, etc. So far, we can see that miscommunication is a beast with one purpose—to destroy communication. We must not let this happen; if we do let it happen, the future generations are doomed, and we better believe it. If we take time to look around us without having to go far, we can see the tensions between parents and their children, men vs. men, women vs. women, men vs. women, husband vs. wives, brothers vs. brothers, sisters vs. sisters, brothers vs. sisters, cousins vs. cousins, uncles vs. nephews, aunts vs. nieces, pastors vs. pastors, priests vs. priests, and neighbors vs. neighbors. The only thing I have learned from all this is that we all guilty of miscommunication. This is certainly not the end of the world. There is a possibility to develop positive and effective communication simply just by learning how to talk and write clearly without complication, by using simple words in that nation's native language that is usually used and understand by the people.

Miscommunication is a poison for the world, especially in the American society. The proof is right under our nose. Communication is dead at a dinner table or at a long ride because everybody is hooked on their phone and their phone only. What an addiction! It is sad to see that families are sitting at a table, having dinner or breakfast, and nobody is talking. Their phones don't give them that permission, isn't that sad? How can we get rid of such nightmare? Can we shift communication to a gear that will influence the American society and the world? Compassion, understanding, mindful awareness, and wisdom may be the only chance to transform such nightmare into living reality. And that's exactly what I do in my house, no phone at the dinner table, period. No phone while we're on a family trip. Let us communicate. That is the proper way to do it if we really want to put family first. If we really want to transform the quality of our communication and erase miscommunication in our lives for good, we have to start communicating more and start working on the quality of our listening. A good listener can reach the highest level of communication. When we listen deeply, we understand; and when we understand perfectly, then we can communicate effectively. If we don't practice mindfulness of understanding, we won't be able to concentrate and listen for long. When we listen with compassion and understanding, that's when deep listening lands to add fuel in the tank of communication so we can communicate better with no misunderstanding. When we don't listen to ourselves with mindfulness understanding, there is a fair chance to lose the ability to listen very well. As human beings, we are full of rage, anger, hate, accusation, and bitterness. These feelings are feelings of wrong perceptions.

Mindfulness is necessary. If we don't practice it, those negative feelings will instill in our mind and bring irritation and frustration into our lives. Brothers and sisters, we communicate to each other in order to understand and to be understood; therefore, we must communicate with passion and effectively. If we are communicating to someone or ourselves and no one is really listening to us or us listening to ourselves, know that we are miscommunicating, or we are communicating with no passion or effectively. Communication taught us that they are two keys that open the door of effective communication:

- Deep listening
- Understanding

These are the only two keys that I know that can open the door to establish effective communication between romantic partners, family members, friends, groups, etc. As humans, we feel great when we are understood, when talking or having a conversation with somebody, especially if we refuse to listen to ourselves and others. For many of us, we think it's a one-way street in our state of mind and always want to be in the front role so we can talk first and expect others to understand us immediately. We don't know it's all about deep listening, not talking in order to create the impact of effective communication. We have to practice deep listening first. When we listen to each other with understanding, that is deep listening that we are putting into play. When you listen to others mindfully, you don't get caught in passing judgement to what they told us or what they are going through because mindfulness/awareness is present in our mind and has no room for negativity. Instead, our awareness will put a smile on the talker's face. He will see that somebody is listening and really care, and he will feel understood, which will make him happy. Deep listening and understanding can change lives and bring some happiness to the heart and make it smiles. Therefore, when you listen deeply to someone talking or communicating; you're just avoiding miscommunication and confusion. That is the way to go if you really want to kick miscommunication out of the curve.

Mindful Breathing

When we inhale and exhale, we calm down our nervous system. When we control our breathing, we not only reduce stress and increase alertness and boost our immune system. But we're also digging deeper and deeper into our understanding while pulling out the best and effective way to communicate. And when we breathe in, breathe out, that's also a way to promote or to call in concentration and improve vitality.

It leaves us with a clear mind and thought so we can do our thing in a more positive way. All I can say is that, this practice is real, and anybody can benefit from it. When we concentrate or meditate or focus on our breathing, we just pick up our phone and give mindfulness a ring. We cultivate mindfulness. What we are really doing is focusing in our breathing, mindful breathing. It will certainly help us to focus more and more on our breathing throughout our daily life. This is the best remedy there is to deal with stress, negative feelings, emotions, and anxiety and will definitely cool us down when we are overheated. As human beings, we are just like an overheated vehicle that needs to be STOPPED, parked, and cool ourselves down when our temperature goes up.

Experts do believe that "a regular practice of mindful breathing can make it easier to do it in difficult situations." When we are able to manage our stress the way we should or properly, we are not only reaching for a better health but also our well-being. Mindfulness is a wonderful thing. It enhances our concentration, performance, improves our understanding, communication skills, and self-awareness. It also promotes relaxation for the body, mind, and soul. It can even help us sleep better for a healthier life.

Mindfulness should be everyone's guardian angel that would guide them to a better living. This guardian angel would also have for duty to shift our attention from whatever it focuses on to the act of taking a precious moment to breathe deeply, which would contribute meaningfully to managing our stress and emotion. Stress is easy to come by, especially when we have a lot in our mind and a lot to deal with; therefore, we become loaded with emotion and triggers frustration. That's exactly why we need to take time out so we can purposefully concentrate (mindful thinking) on something just to clear our mind and thought. It's all about helping our thinking part of our brain to catch up with our emotion part so we can think and act in a positive way without any stress and emotion. Please start living the life you deserve (stress-free life).

Negative Attitude

Negative attitude is a destructive feeling, very bad for our health. Negative attitude is like driving a car at high speed with no breaks, imagine that. Nobody wants to have a conversation with anyone with a stinky attitude. With such attitude, no one wants to be near you or have anything to do with you at all. It's impossible to live a happy and healthy life with a negative attitude. It's like putting lemon in milk, and you know they don't go together. Trust me, you can't take a stinky attitude with you anywhere because the minute people see you, they start walking away from you as far as possible, and that's sucks, doesn't it?

Attitude is everything. It tells people about your manners and who you really are. When you are a negative person, with a negative attitude, you will experience a lot of health-related problems such as stress, depression, low self-esteem. and feelings of hopelessness. Everyone, without any exception, experience negative thoughts from time to time. Most importantly, it's how we are responding to such negative feeling so it doesn't affect our attitudes in a destructive way. The minute we experience negative thoughts. It doesn't matter how long it last; it will flip over our table of "positive attitude" to the other side of "negative attitude" without realizing it. Now it all depends on how we are responding to this negative feeling that is affecting our attitudes. The best motivation to have in such situation is to communicate positively and clearly to ourselves (self-talk) because the message that we are sending to ourselves in that state of mind can be healthy or unhealthy, healthy if we get out real quick of the negative mood and convey it into positive (and that's exactly where we will hold the hand of our happiness and well-being), unhealthy if we stay in the negative mind-set (it will have a negative impact in our health and our attitudes). It will stress us out and reduce our confidence, lower our potential, make us feel unhappy, angry, and ultimately sabotage our dreams and success. Sometimes, we have to learn how to let go our negative thoughts and emotions if we want to live a happy and healthy life. Live healthy and die healthy.

Please avoid people with negative attitudes because they will always try their best to keep you down, believe me. No matter how hard you try, they will repeatedly tell you "you won't make it," "you won't succeed," "it's impossible," "you will never get there," "you are crazy if you think you can achieve this," "there's no way it will happen," "you are not good enough," "you are going to fail," "this is not for you," "you don't have what it takes."

They think they know exactly what is good for you and what is not, what you can do and what you can't do. Who wants to be around these kinds of people? They didn't go anywhere or accomplished anything in their lives. Therefore, they are making sure that anyone that walks on their path don't move forward as well, and that's exactly their objective. So if you fall into their trap, it means that they are smarter than you. In the same token, there are some people who are saying the same exact negative things to themselves too. They STOP their own train that was going at a high speed to their "destination" or "destiny" for no reason at all. Without getting off the STOP they needed to get off so they could accomplish great things in their lives, they messed-up big time. Putting your breaks on or engaging yourselves in habitual negative thoughts is like preparing your own poison and drinking it—meaning, you just commit suicide, unfortunately. Why would anybody do something like that? Why even put yourself in such predicament? Why in the world some of us choose to surrender ourselves to people who only know how to put us down?

People with such state of mind are their worst enemy. Wake up, people, and take a grip of yourselves and your lives. "Experts say, it's the way we choose to relate to our circumstances that makes the experience positive or negative. Such choice can instantly make us stronger or weaker, happier or gloomier, empowered or victimized." Some of us become very negative with a stinky attitude related to our past. We are stuck in our past like we have crazy glue under our feet. It's a must to learn from our past, but it doesn't give us any authorization to be stuck on it. Often, life circumstances or problems can haunt us down wherever we go and prevent new doors from opening on our path because we will lose faith and blindfold us so we don't see new opportunities. What happened, happened. And it's not easy to change the past, but what we can do is change our lives.

It means that we should try our best to see things differently and strive to do better. That's when we are going to feel the power, the power to feel in control and in charge of our lives. I highly recommend to my readers to communicate with themselves from time to time. If you do that in a positive manner, it will take you to the right state of mind (mindfulness), and from there, everything is going to be just fine. Trust and believe. People with stinky attitudes are everywhere—in the churches, work places, in the families, on the buses, at schools, in restaurants, in the super markets, on the street, in organizations, in meetings, etc. It's like a pandemic that's destroying the world little by little just like a deadly cancer. The sad part is that they think the power is in their hands. But today, I am telling them that they are wrong because the real power is in the hands of the positive people with positive attitudes. And these individuals with their stinky attitudes can be very controlling, manipulative, and very intimidating. That's one of the reasons why they think they are powerful no matter how weak they really are.

There are many different strategies, as positive people, that we can use to stay on top of our game. Learning how to communicate effectively so we can handle them with no problem is one of them. People with stinky attitudes carry with them a lack of understanding and mindfulness. They don't understand or refuse to understand that they represent a big problem for themselves and other people. Why is this lack of understanding? Well, it's simple. It's because of their lack of mindfulness that their stinky attitude becomes an obstacle that affects their interactions with others and themselves.

When negative people have a bad experience or something terrible that happened in their lives or to people they care about, they take it to heart and stay as a nightmare into their daily lives and can also take it as an inerasable tragedy. Therefore, they take it will hard on themselves and other innocent people. They think little and talk down on themselves. Most of the time, they turn to drugs and alcohol for help. Instead of finding help, they make matters worse; they find self-destruction. Drugs and alcohol don't bring solutions at all. It just takes you and put you to another mood call "cool" for a minute, and then here you go again. Your problems didn't solve, and on top of that, you become a drunk and a drug addict. So as you can see, drugs and alcohol don't help or heal pain and suffering. Instead, they create more problems. They are the devil, and they only know how to destroy. When you find yourselves in a negative mood, find someone to communicate with, someone that will listen to you with compassion and understanding. Also open your mind for new ideas and new constructive thoughts, even new friends, so you can turn your lives around. Try your best to live your lives with positive attitudes by thinking positively and acting positively. By doing so, you will have a better chance to become new people with new attitudes so success can be reachable. In most cases, anybody who chooses hate over love, depressed and angry at themselves and at other people over any little things instead of choosing joy and happiness, without a doubt, in my mind, will develop a stinky attitude. And trust me, I know it's not easy to enjoy life when everything you do seems to turn against you. When you don't have a job or the one that you have don't pay enough and you can barely eat and pay your bills and find yourselves in a hard situation, it's not easy; I have been there, so I know. I also know that it's hard to smile and keep a positive attitude, but believe me, it's worth it to try. Have conversations with others that will make you laugh and enjoy life while forgetting all of your problems; I call it the "mental exercise for the mind." It will put you in another state of mind or mood and make sure that you forget about the past for a better tomorrow. It's always good to look at things in a different perspective or a different angle for better results.

If anyone has a problem and doesn't look for solutions, the same problem will repeat itself over and over again or will stay with you and never leaves. The worst thing you can do is complain about it; otherwise, you are going to keep punching yourselves in the face; find some solutions instead. It's very important, brothers and sisters, that you seize the power of control so you can be in control of your thoughts, emotions, and actions in the most difficult times. Knowing how to react to these important feelings is crucial. If anyone is able to control his thoughts and actions in any situation, it means that the destiny and the future of that person is also under his control, and that's a fact. Therefore, greatness is waiting for that particular person in every area in his life; that's so awesome, isn't it? We, as humans, have the power to listen deeply to our thoughts and control our emotions, to even communicate with them from time to time, so we can do wonderful things and achieve greatness. What I would like my readers to understand is that wherever negativity is present, positivity is there also; and wherever positivity is present, negativity follows. In every negative situation, there's positivity in that same range, vice versa. It's up to each one of us to know how to deal with them and how we are going to use them to our own and other people's advantage. That's power to us to control our emotions and thoughts. By having such power, you will bring positivity, confidence, and your attitude will change for the better—sweet, isn't it? Whatever happened in your life or whatever tragedy visited you, don't consider yourself as a victim, rather as someone that will take charge and actively engage in making things better, just like a real soldier. A soldier is a real patriot, who takes engagement to protect his country by any means necessary. Therefore, be your own soldier. Stand up for yourself and your rights, and make sure you kick the butt of pain in suffering like a real soldier would so they don't make your life a living hell or miserable with a stinky attitude. A person with a stinky attitude always ends up lonely. They never get far in life. They live alone and die alone because no one wants to be around them with such attitude.

Victimization is not a ghost. It's real. So if you don't take action to find real solution, you will always be a victim that will embrace pain and suffering from circumstances beyond your control. Your attitudes will always suck, bitterness, stinky, helplessness, and that's nasty. You are a soldier of your attitudes, thoughts, and actions. Ultimately, they are the only important assets in your life or career that you have the power to control, so make it happen, and take control of your life. It's true that you might not have any control on some destructive thoughts do to a tragedy that you have no control over, but it's not impossible and it will never be impossible to control your attitudes, thoughts and actions. Such power is within you, and it's yours and yours only. You shouldn't give it away or pass it on to anyone.

Here are four components of Vautoir's wall of good intentions that I'm sharing with you.

- Be a volunteer. Try to help others that are struggling with pain and suffering due to a tragedy. By helping them, you are helping yourself.
- Talk with a positive person that you know that can help, make you see and understand things differently, new ideas, new perspective, new life, and new you.
- Do not concentrate too much on the past. Let it go. It can only make matters worse. Find something fun and enjoyable to do.
- Keep thinking positively, and I assure you that it will take you to your journey. And you will have a better connection with your emotions, goals, and values.

Say to yourself now, "I am not a victim. I am a soldier, a soldier" that will take control of his life to make it better. A soldier that will pass all pain and suffering behind and live life to the fullest, a soldier with positive thinking, attitudes, and actions, that's a real soldier, a soldier with positive result. Thanks, God, for the real "soldier" that I am.

Best communication ever when you can communicate with yourself so you can meet with "mindfulness" that will help you cross the bridge so you can find yourself on the other side of communication. I know for a fact that it's not easy to get rid of stinky attitudes. But who in the world wants or chooses to spend the rest of their life with such a destructive behavior where they think only about hate, anger, and intolerance? It's way much better and healthier to focus on more positive and enjoyable things that will instill in you a positive attitude. Yet despite this positive thinking, but let us not forget that the world we are living in runs by two forces, good and evil. Good is the force that brings light into our lives so we can see where we are putting our feet when walking, and also so we don't bump our heads in the dark. It also put us in the right mind-set to do the right thing.

In the first category, are the positive people, kind, respectful, righteous, honest, loyal, happy, understandable, responsible, tolerant, good-hearted people that believe in God and want to help others by any means necessary?

In the second category: Are the evil people who choose to walk in the dark while serving the devil. They choose to be the devil's little toys and rugs so he can play whenever he wants to and step on and rub his feet whenever he feels like it. These individuals will do all sorts of evil things to others and strongly believe that it's okay because they are heartless and believe there's no God. They found their happiness in making others suffer and taking advantage of them, and don't mind if they go to hell. They are the devil's children because their souls belong to him. It doesn't matter how much they have. They always unhappy and always want more. These individuals, for real, don't know any other way (negative people with negative attitudes) very angry, bigoted, arrogant, belligerent, violent, dishonest, disloyal, critical, hostile, jealous, prejudiced, irresponsible, rude, selfish, greedy, and ignorant people. Please stay away from them for your own good.

Effects of a Negative Attitude

- A negative attitude can stress you out and take you on a ride to meet with depression that will take you and drop you in the world of loneliness, which will be your own little world for the rest of your life.
- A negative attitude can change the way you look and see other people and the world and STOP you from doing things that once you loved to do for fun. Please don't throw away your happiness.
- A negative attitude will make you think very low of yourself. It will make you think that you are nobody. It will take away all your positivity, energy, and motivation to do well in life.
- It will STOP you from reaching the level you want to be at.

Experts say "From a physical standpoint, unhappiness and stress weakens the immune system. When this happens, you can become susceptible to many diseases, from the common cold to chronic pain." Brothers and sisters, life is what we make of it; and the kind of choices that we make every second, every minute, and every hour counts. When it comes to attitudes, the choice is ours. We can choose to have a positive attitude, but in the same token, we can also choose to have a negative one; whatever feeds our needs. It doesn't matter what day it is in the week or on what side of the bed that you roll out. It can be the right side or the wrong side. It doesn't matter in what mood you have chosen to position yourself for the day. It can be a good mood or a bad one. It's up to you. You can make a conscious decision to wake up positively and settle into a beautiful and happy day. In the other hand, you can choose to position yourself into a miserable, angry, stressful, ignorant, depress, and stinky-attitude day. Know that you have the power to make it better for yourself by making the right choice, and do your best to position yourself in the right mood or state of mind (mindfulness). Have a wonderful and blessed day.

My Personal View on Negative People

Negative people are people that are living their lives with pain and suffering. They need all kind of support they can get, especially from positive people so they can change their negative attitudes, thoughts, and actions into positive. We need to listen to them with open ears, compassion, and understanding. A lot of them have been bullied, cheated on, beaten up, betrayed, and lied to. Therefore, they need our assistance because it's not necessarily their fault. It's how they been treated by other people and society that turn them into negative people. We need to learn to treat others with respect by thinking about what we are saying and doing to them before it's too late. Treating them with compassion, understanding, and respect is the only cure to such disease (Vautoir's antidote).

It's really not fair to bring judgement upon them. We have no clue of what they went through in their lives. It's not for no reason when God says "do not judge." He knows that we are incapable of doing so. Any little thing can turn a positive person into a negative person and a negative one into a positive one. STOP passing judgement so quickly. Negative people are like a "derail train." And a "derail train" is a train that accidently leaves its tracks. Therefore, the trail is diverting from its intended course. So all we have to do as human beings is bring our help and our support to these people and see how we can put them back on track. That's mindfulness. That's what righteous, good-hearted people who use their common sense do. They refuse to make others suffer. They bring help and solution to other people's problems.

Please be more helpful to one another, and God is going to bless us abundantly. The most important people on this earth are those who come out of the ordinary to help those in need. When communicating with others, make sure that we choose our words carefully. When using words with our surroundings, make sure that they are not offensive while measuring the impact that it's going to have on people. Always ask yourselves these two valuable questions:

* Is it suitable?
* What will be the impact?

When finish asking ourselves these two questions, it will surely and assuredly help us to control our tone and our body language so we don't offend the person or group that we are talking to. It's vital that we work on our communication skills every day so we can become better communicators. Negative language can really damage our communication skills if we don't choose our words carefully while communicating with one another. Negative communication doesn't bring any solution. It's a red card rather than a green one. The worst part is that some of us don't even realize that they are talking negatively and how hurtful it is. With positive thinking that will put us in the right state of mind (mindfulness), negative communication has a chance to convey into positive communication; and the effect will be very rewarding, believe me.

Effects of Negative Communication

- Negative talk is very harmful to the listener or the addresser. It brings about anger, hate, confusion, pain, and suffering.
- If the kind of conversation that you are having is mean and offensive, there will be negative consequences. Therefore, negative consequences can lead to big argument, fight, and word exchange, etc.
- Negative communication can turn into violence. And when violence is present, anything bad can happen.
- Negative thinking can have a deadly impact on communication. With a positive thinking that will offer us positive attitudes on a silver platter, negative communication can change into positive for the sake of pain and suffering of others.
- Negative attitude does not achieve greatness and success, only a positive mind-set does. So why not think and act positively? Negative attitude will slow you down wherever you go just like a car with a flat tire.
- A negative mind-set will lead you to negative thinking and will crush you and your future into little pieces where

nobody is going to recognize you anymore. Therefore, you are going to end up lost, beat up, smashed, and lonely on a little corner all by yourself. And no one is going to help you; it's over for you, so be positive.

"You are what you think you are. You can achieve whatever you want to achieve in life in a positive mind-set."

Double Tongued

I found out "in order to have a double tongued, you have to say one thing to somebody and turn around and say a whole different thing to someone else."

Such person is a hypocrite, saying one thing and doing another. As we know, "a hypocrite is somebody who pretends to have certain beliefs, attitudes or feelings when he or she really doesn't." For example, a hypocrite can say to others, "Please don't eat pork. It's a very bad meat and not healthy at all." It turns out, that pork is his or her favorite meat of all times. That's hypocritical. The idea of having a double tongue is talking with a false tongue, a tongue that can turn people against each other and against yourself. Nobody trust a double tongued or a false tongue. Such individual is not trustworthy because he or she will say anything to make you or him feel good or just to get some attention or a desired response, with no concern whatsoever about whether or not it's the truth. In 1 Timothy 3:8, Paul mentions being double tongued as something that shouldn't be characteristic of a church leader: "Deacons likewise must be dignified, not double tongued, not addicted to too much wine, not greedy for dishonest gain" (ESV). If you know anybody that's double tongued, be aware that person has a lack of personality, dignity, and integrity (things that nobody can buy no matter how rich you are). These are the only three things that we can take to the grave with us, unfortunately.

Those false tongues, or double tongued, take great pleasure in what they are doing or their habit because their strong desire tell them to say whatever someone wants to hear in the present moment.

Making others think that they are good and nice people, they will do anything to make someone happy in the moment so they can get a kiss, a hug, and a handshake or simply tell them thank you would consider as a sufficient-enough reward for a double tongued to feel proud and continue on the path of their devilishness or dysfunctional mind-set. Once the double tongued have received their reward, it will motivate them with, no doubt, to follow through while searching for their next victims. These false tongued have no intention or concern with making other people feel good or happy. A double tongued is a very selfish person who doesn't care about other people's feelings, couldn't care less, and only care about their selfish goals. They know how to plot ways to get what they want, regardless of the repercussions or the cost to other innocent people. These double tongued people never place their wallet where they can reach for it. They will promise you a mention when they know deep inside that they can only afford a one-bedroom apartment. They can even promise you the moon when they know that there's no way for them to reach at such a high level. These people are shameless. They know how to lie, and they are good at it. They are pathological liars and can fool almost anybody with their convincing conversations. False tongues only use convincing words when talking, so be real careful with those deceivers. The devil is a deceiver and a liar, remember that. They are very smooth in what they say. These double tongued don't need any communication classes or skills to communicate effectively. They just use what I call the "convincing communication skills" or "smooth talk." You can be the most cautious person ever and still get swallowed whole by any giant double tongued, believe it or not. Remember Judas Iscariot, the double tongued, and what he did to Jesus Christ our savior, right. Even after he secretly made plans with the Jewish leaders to carry out his betrayal against Jesus Christ, he did continue as a false disciple, joining with the others even at the Passover meal (Luke 22:4–6, 21).

> Whoever desire to love life and see good days, let him keep his tongue from evil and his lips from speaking deceit." (1 Peter 3:10)

STOP pleasing the devil, brothers and sisters. He has nothing good and positive in him. If you are serving him or consider yourselves as his children, know that you are his rug that he cleans his feet and walk all over whenever he decides to. On the other hand, Jesus Christ considers all his children as his precious people, always blesses and protects them from harm and evil. This is the kind of communication that can put both my readers and me to the other side so we can meet and communicate at the highest level. A double tongued takes pleasure in talking in conflicting ways so he or she can get some advantages. Such attitude can cause division, death, violence, and enemies. It can also bring a lot of pain and suffering.

From what I have learned, double tongued can also consider as gossips; however, they can pretend to love and care about someone but bad-mouth that person behind his or her back. A gossip or a double-tongued person always finds a way to decorate or add seasoning to the story so they can obtain a bigger reaction from the person that they're telling the story to. They embellish the story just to make it look fascinating or exciting so the other person can believe what they are saying. For example, a double tongued might happen to invite you to a party, and that day, you couldn't make it for whatever reason. And next time they see you or call you, they will tell you how fun the party was even though it was boring. They will tell you it was crowded when they were only a few people there. They might also tell you that they were some very important people there when they were none. The double tongued will tell you these things to make you regret that you didn't go to the party. What the false tongued wants you to believe is not the reality. That's the job of a double tongued; that's what they do best. They think by having such a negative behavior. They are on top of the world and ahead of everybody else. They can offer prayers that sound so spiritual, make you feel as though after receiving such prayer, that you are very blessed. Unfortunately, it doesn't express the reality of these double tongued hearts. Jesus Christ do condemn people who try to sound spiritual when praying but are filled with pride and deceit (Luke 18:10–14).

Having double tongue will make of you a liar. God doesn't like liars, and all liars will be harshly judged (Revelation 21:18).

Power of the Tongue

As human beings, our tongues are very powerful. Some of us use it to speak righteously and others falsely. Proverbs 18:21 confirm this by saying, "Death and life are in the power of the tongue, and those who love it will eat its fruits." The tongue has the power to build and to destroy as we all know. A tongue can save and destroy lives. It can put together or destroy relationships. A tongue can be deadly if used the wrong way.

If our words are harsh, we will surely destroy. The tongue also has the power to make you rich, poor, famous, to start or end wars, to bless or to curse, to judge, to rise you and to drag you down, to condemned and to praise the Lord. God's intention is for us to use this power to bring glory to his name and advance his kingdom on this planet. He wants us as humans to use our tongue in a positive way and to tell the truth at all times. Unfortunately, Satan the devil wants a piece of the pie. His dream is to keep the ignorant ones in the dark, and make them use toxic words when communicating to others so they can hurt themselves and their surroundings instead of choosing the light for their own good. My question is, how can someone choose darkness over the light? Where's their common sense? Only a positive tongue can submit to the perfect will of God. Let us master the power of our tongue to praise and bless the name of our master and talk in a *mindful way* to others using *empowering words*.

Our tongue is one of the most important parts of our body. If we compare it to other parts of our body, we can say that our tongue is very small, but we rely on it to taste our food and determine if what we are eating is good or not. It allows us to talk, to sing, to taste, etc. Yes, it's true, it's tiny, but it has a huge responsibility as we can see. It's also one of the most dangerous parts of our body. It can cause some pain and suffering. It can heal, destroy, and cause death. When it comes to communicate or having conversation with others, we have wonderful opportunities through that moment to have healthy or unhealthy communication. Either we do well or we end up messing up. If we are mindful, we would make the best of these opportunities. In Colossians 4:6, Paul wrote, "Let it be helpful, and filled with both truth and love."

Brothers and sisters, we can change the world and people around us by moderating our tongue and words (meaning, we have to change ourselves first).

> The tongue is a small thing, but what enormous damage it can do. (James 3:5 TLB)

So our tongue can be a positive, a negative, and a destructive force depending upon the good and bad words that we allow our tongue to launch. Why not make our tongue a respectful tool and a means of success, instead of a destructive force? Tongues have no bones but strong enough to destroy lives. I tell you today, my brothers and sisters, I would rather bite my tongue a thousand times a day instead of hurting and offending someone with it. Our tongue is so powerful as a small flesh. It can destroy almost everything and everybody; therefore be mindful before using it.

How we use our tongue says a lot about us because it reveals a good deal of who we really are. We must be very careful of what we are saying with our tongue. A foolish tongue is a dirty and toxic tongue that utters lies and repeat deceit that will only bring pain and suffering to others, very "inconsiderate people." But a righteous tongue talks wisely and honestly and makes sure that he or she doesn't hurt or harm anybody, "talking with wisdom."

A Lying Tongue

Unfortunately, most of the time, dishonesty is convenient, and honesty becomes inconvenient in the lives of most people on this planet. Most of the time, it's easier to tell a lie than the truth (meaning, it's not easy to tell the truth or admitting to something we have done wrong that can cost us our career). It might mean embarrassment or else.

For example, Jesus Christ never lied even though it would have been more convenient for him. Why can't we be just like Jesus Christ in that way? Tell the truth at all times, even though it can backfire on us. We only tell the truth when it's in our advantage or gain something from it in return. Yet we're often willing to lie when it's in our best interest, but the intelligent man thinks and sees things differently. He always tells the truth no matter what, no matter the outcome and how other people feel or understand it. He will even die for it because he knows the truth hurts, but it will always be and will stay the truth. The wise man does not fabricate lies to avoid the heat of the truth. Most of us, as human beings, take pleasure in stretching the truth to save and better serve us; "let the truth be told." The "dirty tongue" talks harshly, very toxic, and leaves pain and suffering while the righteous tongue speaks respectfully, kindly, and thoughtfully while bringing healing to people around him. People with toxic tongue often don't realize what they said until it's too late. That's why it's imperative to think and talk when we don't think before we talk. We speak out of emotion, not out of righteousness.

Righteous Tongue

The Word of God reminds us as human beings to use words that express nondiscrimination, understanding, compassion, love, forgiveness, and support. It's very liberating to use nontoxic words either by writing, having a conversation, talking and communicating (compassionate tongue). Talking with a clean tongue is a healing not only for the speaker but also for the person or group being spoken to. Be aware that every toxic word used by our tongue that contains harsh words, discrimination, violence, and hate will make us and others suffer.

Please let us get rid of our poison tongue so together we can minimize suffering. It's a very simple equation; dirty tongue causes suffering, but a clean and righteous tongue brings well-being to others. As we know, our tongue has the capacity to heal and to destroy. Why don't we do this right now, right this minute? Why don't we

STOP whatever we are doing? It doesn't matter who we are; you can be a president, a CEO, a manager, a doctor, a nurse, a teacher, a student, a businessman, a bus driver, a truck driver, a child, an adult, a husband, a wife, etc. Please don't wait on this one. Pick up your phone now. Make a phone call, e-mail, or text someone that you have hurt in the past and apologize to that person and be sincere about it by showing remorse. Tell him or her that you were wrong while showing some regrets and taking full responsibility of your wrongdoing. By doing so, you will heal the wounds that you have caused to that person for so many years through pain and suffering. This will be taken in great consideration, and you will help them to suffer less. And God will forgive you.

When our way of thinking changes from negative to positive, it will also help our toxic tongue to be cleaned and turns it into a compassionate tongue. It's a complete renovation from mind to body, and it's also a practice of love and understanding directed to ourselves and others. A righteous tongue will always look for its mistakes and try to correct them. A righteous tongue doesn't hurt anybody's feelings. It talks with respect, compassion, understanding, love, and well-being so it doesn't take the other person out of his or her comfort zone. A righteous tongue will always know what to say, what not to say. It's not the intention of a righteous tongue to hurt anybody's feelings, and it will never be because a righteous tongue speaks with positivity (tongue awareness). Steve Harvey said, "There's power in your tongue, be mindful of the words you speak, focus on positive life affirming words."

God is a lover of the life he created, and he takes pleasure in promoting life, not hate, violence, and crime. A life-giving tongue is like a fountain of life, not a grave. It talks positively compared to a negative tongue that brings only pain and suffering. "The mouth of the righteous is a fountain of life." Righteous people live by true wisdom. When we act like fools, we push away reason; and without proper thinking, we hurt those around us. Let us think wisely before we talk or say anything that can harm those we love and those in our surroundings. Before a wise man engages in any type of conversation whatsoever, he thinks before he talks so he doesn't cause pain and suffering to others. He always ends up making the right decision by saying the right thing (self-control). By having self-control, he can only speak the truth without offending anybody. It's all about how we use our tongue. It's up to us because everything in life has repercussions.

"The mouth of the righteous utters wisdom and his tongue speaks justice" (Psalm 37:30). We don't have to look far nor hard in the Bible to find out it talks a lot about the tongue. It's a tool, a powerful one that every human being possesses. The tongue has the power to do much good; on the other hand, it also has the power to do wrong. Proverbs in the Bible talk a lot about the fool by saying that he will hate your words, but he will not be able to retrain his. It also talks about seeking wise counsel and knowing what's acceptable to say. Life and death lie in the power of the tongue. With our tongue, we bless God but curse our brothers and sisters. Out of the same mouth comes blessings and cursing. May this never be! "The preparations of the heart belong to man, but the answer of the tongue is from the Lord." You may plan on what you are going to say, but it is the Lord who allows what comes out. What's in your heart cannot be hidden. "Out of the abundance of the heart the mouth speaks," and every "idle word" will be judged (Matthew 12:36). But the Bible says, "A righteous man will eat well by the fruit of it" (Proverbs 13:2).

Righteous tongue requires us to be kind and respectful toward others by not saying things that are false or hurting other people's feelings. When acting and talking in such positive manner, we just portray ourselves to a better and shiny light. This way, we will only use "peaceful language" that will make others feel comfortable being around us. Please, brothers and sisters, restrain yourselves from using dirty tongues that are violent, condemning, accusing, humiliating, abusive, and causing pain and suffering to others. Every time we want to say or express some concerns, please be humble and respectful while taking a deep breath to search for a proper way to convey or express what we want to say. If we use or do this practice when talking to other people, we will have the ability to use our tongue in a more effective way that will not cause others to suffer and will help us to express ourselves in a more respectful way and more effectively in our every day life. We can be talking to a family member, a group, a romantic partner, a husband or a wife, a friend, or a coworker. Such practice will give us a deep understanding of what to say and how to say it in any given situation. This focus is not only about respect and how we talk to ourselves and others but also how to connect the mind to the tongue for better results. When we talk in a respectful way to others and tell the truth at all times, compassion arises, and we use "mindful talk" that reflects our respect and good intentions toward others. Instead of talking harshly, we choose to talk with compassion, understanding, and respect. You see, with Vautoir's antidote, everything's to be gained and nothing to lose. It brings us peaceful mind (mindfulness).

Proverbs of a Righteous Tongue

- The mouth of the righteous brings forth wisdom.
- The lips of the righteous know what is acceptable.
- A man's stomach shall be satisfied from the fruit of his mouth.
- From the produce of his lips he shall be filled.
- The heart of the wise teaches his mouth and add learning to his lips.
- A man has joy by the answer of his mouth.
- A word spoken in due season how good it is.
- He who gives a right answer kisses the lips.
- Sweetness of the lips increase learning.
- The tongue of the wise uses knowledge rightly.
- A wholesome tongue is a tree of life.
- The lips of the wise will preserve them.

Proverbs of a Foolish Tongue

- Do not speak in the hearing of a fool, for he will despise the wisdom of your words.
- Any fool can start a quarrel.

- Excellent speech is not becoming to a fool.
- A fool does not take correction. Rebuke is more effective for a wise man than a hundred blows on a fool.
- Even a fool is counted wise when he holds his peace.
- The mouth of fools pour forth foolishness.
- In the mouth of a fool is a rod of pride.
- He who answers a matter before he hears it, it is folly and shame to him.
- A fool has no delight in understanding but in expressing his own heart.
- A fool's mouth is his destruction, and his lips are the snare of his soul.
- In the multitude of words sin is not lacking.
- Go from the presence of a foolish man when you do not perceive in him the lips of knowledge.
- But the folly of fools is deceit.
- A fool's lips enter into contention, and his mouth calls for blows.
- And a fool's voice is known by his many words (ECCL).
- When you make a vow to God, do not delay to pay it, for he has no pleasures in fools (ECCL).

Sharp Tongue

A sharp tongue is a very dangerous tongue that often speaks in a disrespectful or unpleasant way and can cut you to the bone. Talking in such way is the practice of speaking to others in a harsh and insulting manner. Having a sharp tongue in the kind of language we use is like stabbing or shooting others while leaving them with unhealing wounds. Negative or unkind conversation is no different than a sharp knife, a bullet, or a razor blade. Talking to others in an insulting, disrespectful, or harsh manner is very painful. When someone has a sharp tongue, it means that such person says things that are hurtful and unkind to others. We cannot take back what's already said, and that's why we have to be careful of what we say to others.

There's a tongue in every human's mouth. Some of us use it for the right purpose, and some of us don't. Some of us use it to eat, to talk, to sing, and to praise the Lord. Others use it to speak unkindly, to insult others, to lie, to destroy, to bring division, to kill, and to harm others in any way they can. So as we can see, there are two categories of tongues that give us two categories of people, one that practices righteousness and another that practices evil (positive and negative, good and bad, right and wrong). Therefore, we have what we call positive and negative tongue.

Positive Tongue

A positive tongue is a tongue that is righteous and portrays good and positivity. Such tongue uses compassion, understanding, and respect.

Negative Tongue

A negative tongue is a tongue that talks unkindly to others and leave them with pain and suffering. They love to see others suffer, pure evil. A sharp tongue can do more harm than good as we already notice. A sharp tongue will talk without thinking and consideration. Therefore, a sharp tongue can be portrayed as a dangerous weapon. A person with a sharp tongue is quick to judge and talk about others. And the information will speed up at 150 m/h whether it is a fact or false. The impression expressed by these destructive words has the ability to destroy people's personality, dignity, and integrity. They can also cause serious chaos in the society and among people around us just like the fake news does. When a sharp tongue bad-mouths you or say destructive things about someone, a group, or other people, it can only bring negative impression. The minute that the negative impression takes place or strike, there's no going back, innocent or guilty. The negative resulting effects of the sharp tongue are surely that people's feelings are seriously hurt and can destroy lives of innocent people. The sad part is that the person who came up with the white lie, the story, or negative words, however you want to call it, to trigger the fire will, at this point, regret it but cannot take it back for the damages that it already causes. It's proven to us that a sharp tongue can do more harm than good once again. There's a saying in Creole that says "you don't judge a one ear donkey" (meaning, you don't judge one person. you don't bring your judgement on what only one person is telling you). Every story has two sides; therefore, when you hear something about someone or somebody tells you a story about another person, please don't take it to heart and pass it on to others without facts or tangible proof, also without hearing the other person. Only a fool will hear or tell something about someone and instantly, with no proof or contacting the other person, will start judging and pass it on to others. The fool will not look for the other side of the story so he can know if what he hears is true or not. If you don't know the accuser or you didn't see it with your own eyes or heard it with your ears, then don't say anything because you don't know the facts. A wise man will never bring judgement on a rumor or some story that someone told him. He will listen and search for the other side of the story. He will immediately call for his mindfulness to see if what you are telling him is the truth or not because it can be the truth. Also, it can be a white lie, or you can take it out of proportion, who knows (common sense). People can make up stories just to hurt someone that they don't like or jealous of or hate for no reason at all. We're just humans, right? The wise man knows that, but the fool doesn't; therefore, don't be a fool. Be wise.

    Knowing all these pain and suffering that a sharp tongue can bring doesn't mean that it cannot be abridge. What I would suggest to all sharp-tongue people is this: always think before you talk by pausing and reflecting on the repercussions of your stories and lies before you launch them. Also try to take a deep breath while accessing your mind to think about your wrongdoings so you can make others suffer, bring divorce in a family, make someone commit suicide, break up a friendship or relationship, etc. Please think twice before you talk, so you can save a marriage, a life, a romantic relationship, a friendship, etc. May God bless you.

CHAPTER 2

Healthy vs. Unhealthy Marriages and Relationships

A healthy marriage or relationship is when both partners or spouses in such partnership put into play respect, love, care, honesty, wisdom, and support each other no matter what and always tell the truth to each other. It doesn't mean that such relationship or marriage is perfect. There is no such a thing as a perfect marriage or relationship. It is also a way to tell you that nobody is perfect except God. As you know, teeth and tongue are best friends ever, right, but doesn't teeth bite tongue from time to time? And it doesn't mean that they hate each other either. Things happen. It is life. This is to prove to you that there is no such a thing as a perfect romantic relationship or marriage because anything can happen at any given time. It is true though, relationships, no matter what kind, it is has the ability to enrich our lives, even force us to enjoy life. It can be a relationship that brings happiness and joy, and it can also bring harm, tears, and discomfort. If anyone in a relationship wants it to be a healthy one, then both of you should develop a connection base on positivity, seeking for good fuel that can full the tank of such relationship. The good clean fuel would be the followings:

- Respect each other. "Treat me the way you would like to be treated," said God.
- Support each other no matter what the circumstances may be.

- Always tell the truth to each other. It helps relationships and marriages a lot.
- Be fair to each other by what we say and do.
- Be honest to each other at all times.
- Communication is the key, and good and positive communication will keep our relationships and marriages alive and healthy.

All these awesome suggestions take time and demand a lot of work. To keep a romantic relationship or marriage going and healthy, it needs to be maintained. Keep in mind that such strategy falls in the category of all relationships: friendship, family, romantic relationships, etc. If you are in a healthy relationship whatsoever, it should bring you happiness not stress and suffering. Believe it or not, every relationship will have stress at times. It is inevitable because it is something that nobody has control over. But still, we can keep each other happy if we try our best. "Where there is a will, there is a way."

As human beings, we will have various relationships through our lives on this earth. Whether they are intimate relationships, family relationships, friendships, coworker relationships, etc., please be aware that these relationships can be full of positivity and negativity.

Positivity: excitements, happiness, joy, fun, respect, understanding, communication, compassion, wisdom, and love.

Negativity: hate, anger, stress, frustration, emotions, sadness, loneliness, disrespect, cheating, lies, miscommunication, disappointment, and misunderstanding.

The truth of the matter is when we take a close look at relationship, we can notice that it has two faces—right or positive, wrong or negative. We can flip it to the right side or to the wrong side depending on our attitudes, behaviors, and how we conceive things. While relationships can be the best thing that can happen to us in our lives, it can also be the worst nightmare ever because life is all about risks and challenges. Most of us get into a relationship or marriage with someone in a state of mind or a net in hand to capture all negativity of the other person or partner instead of bringing something positive to the table of this marriage or relationship, big mistake. The real purpose of these two elements is to see what goods we can bring in, not what we can capture and hold as bad or negative, and hold them against our partner or lover; that is killing our marriage or relationship. Don't get into a relationship or marriage to change, fix, capture, and hold against your boyfriend, girlfriend, husband, or wife.

Be there to bring solution and positivity like a real role model would do; therefore, be one. We should always search for the quality that we value in our partner or spouse, and if they are not there, make sure that we nourish and water them with the right seed so it can mash up with the ingredients of the healthy relationship that we deserve and after.

First and foremost, the foundation of a healthy relationship or marriage should be based on mutual respect, honesty, and trust. And without these three components, they can't be solid and strong and will not be able to sit on a deep understanding. When it comes to marriage or relationship, it is all about lifting each other as high as possible, not pulling each other down and walk all over one another. We need to grow and strive so we can enjoy our children and life together, and that's exactly where happiness is hiding. And as a couple, let's find it or discover it together; that's very healthy, don't you think? Please STOP assuming in a marriage or relationship. It's not healthy at all. The best thing to do is to communicate with one another so both of you can stay healthy and live life to the fullest.

Differences in Marriages and Relationships

It's mandatory that in a relationship or marriage, both partners and spouses respect the differences of each other, the right to think and act differently, the right to have different views and understanding of things because we are different from one another. Therefore, of course, we are going to have different opinion of things, have different friends, like different things, and activities; it's logical and understandable. But it doesn't mean that we can't come together and be together because of our differences. As a family, romantic partners, husbands, wives, coworkers, friends, etc., we can still accomplish great things together regardless of our differences. It's not impossible; it's achievable. We have to learn how to fight fairly because there will always be disagreements in any relationship or marriage; why? Well, no marriage or relationship is perfect. Each partner or spouse has to be willing to negotiate, communicate, and compromise so together we can ride the train that will drop us on the path of a successful and healthy relationship or marriage. The goal here is to work in a unity to find a common ground where we'll come together for the well-being of our love and children.

Unhealthy and Abusive Relationships

What constitutes an unhealthy relationship? Well, the answer is simple; it's the negative feelings that we develop day by day in such relationship that constitute an unhealthy relationship (unhappy, misunderstood, sadness, hate, anger, lack of trust and respect, violence, blaming, controlling, etc.). When your partner try to put you down and hold you as hostage from your own home, and try to hurt you in any way (physically, sexually, and mentally), know that it's time for you to get out of this unhealthy and violent relationship and look for help, ASAP. Be aware that those violent individuals are full of excuses for their unacceptable behaviors and will say to you from time to time how much they love you and want to be with you; they can't live without you. Or they will let you know that you're fat and ugly even though you are not, and nobody wants you, you are nobody, so you can hold on to them and don't let go. It's just a mind game just to let you believe that you are stuck with them and only them. They will manipulate you in a way so you can do what you've told and force to do what you don't want and like to do. These kinds of people are very good at what they do. They are control freaks. If your partner or spouse is also a control freak, know that you are in trouble, and you have one option—run without looking back until you catch the train of no return. It's not easy and it's impossible to grow and strive in such unhealthy and unhappy relationship. Look for someone you can talk to or communicate with or shoot me an email at jean.paul751@yahoo.com, and I will be glad to help in any way that I can.

I am aware of how hard it is in this world to grow and strive together in a relationship and to keep it healthy with all the violence, cheating, resentment, dishonest, accusations, blaming, lies, shame, fear, financial problems, etc., that are holding us back from finding better ways and solutions for the problems and ugly situations that we find ourselves in. A lot of men and women around the world are very violent in some relationships and marriages because of their past or the way they were raised. As children, they grow up in a very disturbing environment where they were abused sexually, physically, and mentally. They didn't have a voice that could stand up for them and protect them, no rights, no love, and no respect for them; therefore, it's very hard, if not impossible, for these kinds of people to understand or know anything at all about love and healthy relationships and marriages. When children grow up around such negative behaviors where they are yelled at and abused, they automatically think that's normal or that's how things should be. In their state of mind, they think that's how every family should relate to each other because that's all they see and know. So as they are growing up and becoming young adults, they have to learn as they are growing to reach that stage because they have been there living their lives with this unacceptable abuse, and disrespectful behavior doesn't make it normal.

It's not the way to treat or relate to others; new ways can be taught, how to talk and communicate to each other the right way, also how to handle conflicts or arguments without hurting the adversary in any way. Some of you may think that these sufferers can learn through their partners or friends, and everything is going to be okay—well maybe, maybe not. The reason why I said that is because great damage has been done, and that's why it would be better for them to see an expert in that matter for better result, especially when they turn to drugs and alcohol. Then again, it's just my opinion. It's true that lessons can be learned in positive conversations or communications and change or turn someone's life forever. There's a possibility that it can happen to these sufferers also if they are taught about mutual respect and love. And I will encourage anybody who needs help to seek for it. It's not a bad thing.

Here are two reasons why most people who stay in a violent relationship stay in such relationship or marriage.

- Violence in a relationship is a cycle because it goes away for a period of time. And somehow the victim thinks it's gone forever, and it will not come back anymore but always comes back when least expected. Such anomaly will pass on from generation to generation because unfortunately it's a lesson well taught by the parents who practice it and well learned by the innocent children in such environment.
- People do get caught up in this cycle of violence because they think for one reason or the other even though they don't stand up against it. It will somehow vanish because, in their mind, they think if the violence stops for a few minutes, everything is going to be fine again. No, it's not until you reach for help or get out of there. Also unless you see the person who practice violence on you and your children is willing to change and learn how to deal with his or her anger and frustration that's causing such nightmare.

Be aware that this deadly cycle will always repeat itself until you do something about it. It's an awesome thing when you can redirect your thinking, actions, attitudes, and behaviors. Jesus Christ loves you.

Controlling behavior

Controlling behavior is when a friend, a wife, a husband, a coworker, a family member, and a romantic partner expects you to compel and to boss you around. Such individual think he or she has the power and the remote control of your life in hands, just like a TV remote where he or she can change the channel, put up or down the volume, or turn on or off the TV whenever he or she pleases.

What he or she doesn't understand is that you're not a TV set. You are human beings just like him or her. Their goal is to dominate and control their partner. Those cowards used force and abusive languages to gain power and total control over their partner, and that's the only reason why they use violence. They don't know anything or just don't care about fairness. They use fear and intimidation so they can hold on to their power to control and keep walking all over their partner.

Exclusion

In order for the abuser to keep/maintain the power and the control of the other person and the relationship or marriage, the first thing he will do is to exclude his partner from all decision-making like she's nonexistent, just like a ghost, so his partner can feel like she's not important and unwanted. The abuser wants his partner to have as minimal contact as possible with others (isolation). You're present physically, but in reality, for them, you are not because they act like you are not here at all. It's a great way to control somebody by keeping her from exercising any rights or having an active voice from her own life and from her family. Also the abuser will control her financially, either through how much money she should have or having her give him her pay check or mostly tell her how she should spend her money and how much she should spend.

If you find yourself at home unemployed or "house wife," some abusers will leave you broke forever, and others will give you a small amount just enough for you to buy yourself some candy—that's if you like candy. If by any chance you are allowed to keep your pay check, they will keep track of every financial transaction that you made. That is another form of power and control just to keep you unhappy and unhealthy, making your life miserable.

Blame

The offender will blame you for all of his unacceptable behaviors. He will tell you in a minute "it's because of you or what you did that make me act in that way so it is your fault not mine," and they are very good at what they do. The blaming is also another form of control, manipulation, and power; therefore, be aware.

If any of these signs that I reveal today resonate to you or if you find yourself, a friend, a family member, a coworker or someone that you know is in an abusive relationship or marriage, please reach out for help. There is a lot of professionals and counselors out there that can help. If you choose to stay in such relationship because of love or the sake of the children, I would encourage you to set some boundaries. But on the other hand, if you choose to leave, help yourself with some prayers for all these emotions and pain and suffering that will arise from this difficult decision of yours. May the Lord be with you.

Wisdom

It is imperative that we bring some common sense into our relationships and marriages by adopting the Word of God in our relationships or marriages so they can be at a minimum and so we can treat the other person like we would like to be treated, at the same time apply some wisdom and compassion to save our relationships. Too many children around the world are affected by this pandemic call, "divorce or break up." As adults, we need to reason more and start valuing our children because as parents, we are causing them too much pain and suffering coming from our relationships or marriages that's always heading for disaster. It is time to say enough is enough and find real solutions to our problems so we can be and stay together to save the children. May God guide our relationships and marriages for the sake and well-being of the children.

Abusive relationships or marriages can be a nightmare. It can happen to anyone. It doesn't pick and choose. It doesn't matter if you are rich or poor, men or women, and your ethnic background, etc., none of that. More importantly, what everybody should know is that abusive behavior, wherever it comes from, is unacceptable, period. Anybody in an intimate relationship or married should feel respected, happy, valued, safe, and loved because we deserve it as human beings. In a violent intimate relationship or marriage, people always think about physical damage, or should I say people have a tendency to value more the physical damage without focusing on the emotional and psychological effects that are way more severe. This nightmare violence can destroy any sufferer's self-worth, lead to depression and anxiety, and leave them with a negative feeling of loneliness and helpless.

No human being should endure this kind of pain and suffering, and if you find yourself in an abusive relationship or marriage and you want out or break free, first you have to recognize that you are in danger, and it's a matter of life or death and you really need help. Then you can start looking for help right away. Time's up.

Here are eighteen signs of an abusive relationship or marriage from Vautoir's wall of good intentions that will help anyone to determine whether their relationship or marriage is abusive or not.

- When you're scared talking to your partner or your lover by thinking you might get yelled at or beaten.
- When in your state of mind, you think you deserve all the screaming, beatings, and pain and suffering.
- When you feel as though there's nothing you can say or do to please your partner.
- When you wonder all the time or keep asking yourself if something is wrong with you.
- When you pick and choose what to say what not to say in a conversation out of fear so you don't get your partner angry.
- When you can't stop criticizing yourself and feel that you are nobody but a low life.
- When you feel emotionally helpless and lonely in your own little world created by you.

- When your partner screams and humiliates you in front of his friends or your friends or in front of his family members.
- When your partner treats you with no respect and you see that the love is no longer there.
- When you never say or do anything right and never value your opinion or accomplishments and ignore you as much as he or she can.
- When your partner keeps blaming you for every little thing even for his or her abusive behavior.
- When your partner sees you as an asset and a sex object just to cover his or her needs rather than as a lover or someone they have fallen in love with.
- When your partner chooses to violently rip you instead of making love to you.
- When your partner can't control his or her temple.
- When your partner threatens to hurt or kill you if you decide to leave one day.
- When your partner wants to know where you are at all times and who you're with and constantly check on you.
- When your partner holds you hostage, can't see your friends nor family members and can't even go to church or to school.
- When your partner is always in your phone to see who you talked to and reading all your text messages.

Hopefully, these signs are helpful and will guide you to make the best decision toward your relationships and marriages and make you see and understand what you did not. Always look for a way to save yourself in an abusive relationship or marriage because it's a matter of life-or-death situation. It's all about you, and it will always be. And make sure that you ask God for help. He's here to help, and he wants the best for you.

Mind Game in Romantic Relationships

The mind game is a way for the gamer to gain power and total control over the other person in a relationship or marriage. Basically, what they will do is to create confusion in your mind by making sure that you denied your own reality by denying everything you confronting them about. For example, they can say something like, "From now own, I am going to keep my promise." But when you confront that particular person about it, he will deny he ever said that in the first place. It's just a way to put your two feet in one shoe so you can be totally off balance so you can doubt your own self and perception and leave you in the dark side of the reality of things and confused. If you find yourself in such relationship, it's super urgent and important to get help, and set some really clear boundaries. And give it a serious thought to really know if that's the kind of relationship you deserve, want to be in, be happy and healthy; peace be with you.

How to Improve Our Relationships and Marriages

In order to improve our relationship status, firstly, we need to want to change first by changing our way of thinking and acting, the way we talk and treat each other, etc. Secondly, before we jump into a relationship or get married to someone, get to know that person first. I know we all get excited, want to have somebody to marry to have fun, pleasure, a future, and children with. But if we make this terrible mistake, "don't take time to know that person," what is going to happen is that we are going to discover lots of things in that person that we may not be pleased with, such as a lot of bad habits, attitudes, and many unacceptable behaviors that will turn you off, just like a light switch, while thinking that we were going to have an awesome relationship together. And that is exactly why a lot of people STOP putting great effort over a period of time in their relationship or marriage because they feel as though it is going to drop-dead. If we're really looking forward to have long-lasting relationships or marriages, our intentions have to be good and positive. It is that simple.

Know how to choose because your own choice can turn your life, and your future into a nightmare. Be positive at all times, don't lie to each other, don't cheat, be honest, be loyal, be fair, be compassionate and respectful, and always show gratitude. Then only then we will have an inseparable life together. I know it's easier to said than done, I am married myself so I know, but with a little effort, and good will we can go a long way.

I strongly believe that these 4 positive intentions bellow can change any marriage or relationship for the better, it will improve it and raise the bar so it can reach the level of happiness and healthy.

Respect

Everybody wants to be respected and deserve to be. That's why you should be a role model to others, especially to your partner or spouse in that sense. By showing respect, he or she will reproduce it back to you. How awesome is that?

Compassion

Always show compassion toward our partner or spouse so we can ease their pain and suffering. That will give them more faith to believe in us, and such strategy will bring hope in our relationship or marriage. Where there is hope, there is life, and such intention will strengthen both components.

Attention

Who doesn't like attention? Know that our partner or spouse always been seeking for our attention just like a baby. Therefore, show them that they are not unwanted. They are important and needed so they can understand that our focus is on them. Such treatment will bring warmth into their heart, and they will feel and see the change.

Here is the pick: choose one day of the week to spend some time together with no interruption and destruction, and that will be our own little world with no cell phones, no TV, no one else but us.

Gratitude

It is imperative that we show some appreciation to our partner or spouse because a "lack" of gratitude will sink any good relationship or marriage because the person in question will feel not appreciated. A thank you, a hug, and a kiss from time to time will keep both partners and spouses happy and healthy. Not only that we show appreciation for what they do but also for what they forget to do or don't take interest of doing; gratitude wins either way.

Let us let positivity be our rolling stone so in a togetherness, we can create or build a chain of positivity to save our relationships and marriages for the sake and the well-being of the children around the world. Even for the sake and well-being of our relationships and marriages, why not?

Here are twenty progressive steps to a better marriage or relationship from Vautoir's wall of good intentions that I'm sharing with you.

- When you need to discuss a conflict, do it when neither one of you is angry or tired.
- Express kindness, compassion, affection and appreciation at all times.
- Always show that your partner's or spouse's feelings matters.
- Never be afraid to apologize when you are wrong.
- Show love and respect even when you disagree.
- Avoid harsh words, be positive toward each other in your say and actions.
- Avoid talking at the same time; learn to listen and then talk.
- Be reasonable, compassionate, and understanding.
- Keep a positive attitude at all times.

- Create time to be with your partner or spouse; it's imperative.
- Be committed and devoted to each other.
- Be respectful of one another.
- Try to eliminate any accusation without tangible proof.
- Adopt the Bible truths that strengthen relationships.
- Promote only true love and affection.
- Keep quiet and listen when your partner is talking.
- Open your ears wide so you can hear (deep listening).
- Be trustful and respectful to your partner or spouse!
- Always give your partner or spouse some attention.
- Stay focused and keep eye contact when he or she is talking; it will tell him or her that you care.

Show Respect

The harsh words that you hitting your romantic partner with can be hurtful. It can cause a lot of pain and suffering. It doesn't matter how mad or angry you are. You have to have the ability to control what is coming out of your mouth. When you show respect to your partner or spouse, they will return the favor (reproduction). Why treat or talk to someone or your partner in a way that you wouldn't want him or her to talk to you? It's more than time to start talking in a positive way and with respect to each other so your relationship can move forward so it can meet with its journey.

It doesn't mean that we are not going to make mistake, this is not what I am saying. It is something that we cannot prevent because it is in our DNA (our blood); therefore, there is nothing that we can do about that. But what we can do is start treating each other with respect, understanding, and compassion for a healthier relationship or marriage. We all know how hurtful it is when our romantic partner or spouse speaks harshly to us which is very toxic for our health; therefore, let us be positive in every situation in life that we are facing.

The Truth in Relationships

STOP turning and twisting the truth around. The truth is the truth, so be it. Let the truth be free in your relationship, especially in your romantic relationships and marriages. What you need to know is that the truth is a deep foundation for long and lasting relationships. Any relationship that does not build on such foundation, the truth will crumble and fall. Any solid relationship is based on the truth, period.

We should tell the truth at all times so our romantic partner, friend, husband, or wife, etc., don't catch us in our white lies. Let us free ourselves from such embarrassment. It is imperative to tell the truth no matter what the consequences may be. But knowing how to lay the truth is something else. Don't say it in a way to cause pain and suffering to the other person. Use compassion (right or wrong). It doesn't matter, we just have to be professional about how we tell the truth. We don't have to say it in a harsh way and say "well, we are just telling the truth." Do we really know that what we consider as the truth may not be the whole truth? Therefore, be careful of what we are saying and how we say it. Also what we believe that is true might be a white lie so use caution so we don't hurt innocent people. Show some respect for the truth. Don't use it with harsh words. Use compassion and wisdom instead when telling the truth. We have to do our best to find the way to tell the truth without putting the other person in his little shoe and feel threatened. It's always in someone's best interest to tell the truth in a loving and protective way as I have learned. What we consider as the truth can be filled of our own perception. Be mindful of our words while searching for the best way to launch them so they don't turn out to be a destructive missile. Our words can be a bomb full of toxins, or it can be "Vautoir's antidote." The choice is yours. When we tell the truth with compassion and kindness, the other person will receive it with ease and love. Is life really that complicated? Why not make it easier on ourselves and others? Not only we will benefit from it but so does our children and the society that we're part of. This is the truth, nothing but the truth, so help me God. When we talk using harsh and toxic words, we are causing great pain, and most of the times, not easy to heal.

If we communicate with compassion and understanding, trust me, we will cause less damage, not only for the listener but for the communicator also. Why make a brother or sister suffer needlessly? Why don't we use positivity in what we say by using compassion and understanding? It doesn't matter how truthful what we're saying can be. Respect comes first in everything. Plus, we are humans after all. Why not showing each other love and respect for a better world?

When we are having a conversation with somebody, even though we have to tell the truth, be moderate and compassionate when telling the truth without having to hurt the other person's feelings. I know some of us will say it in a way to cause pain and suffering and say, "Well, I just say it the way it is." It doesn't matter if we are telling the truth or not, we can still say it in a respectful manner (mindful awareness). Life is too short. Let us make the best of it by treating others with respect, love, and consideration. I highly recommend "Vautoir's antidote" for a better generation and better world. Look around us, and see what we are doing to the children as adults. Are we telling them the truth, nothing but the truth? Of course not, we lie to them every second, every minute, and every hour. We need to tell the truth and communicate in a positive way around our children as responsible parents. Telling them the truth will give them as obligation to tell you the truth also. We lie to them; they will lie to us. We lie to our friends, romantic partners, husbands and wives, they will also lie to us. What you do, you get. Let us start by telling the truth.

Poor Communication in Marriages and Relationships

Without communication in a relationship or marriage, it's almost impossible to understand each other and keep this relationship or marriage going in the right direction to its journey. It will create resentment and make each one of you think that you don't want each other. None of you know what's going on into each other's head in a romantic relationship or marriage. That's why it's extremely important to communicate with one another so you can be on the same page for the sake of what you have going on. In a romantic relationship or marriage, you should not keep distance between one another; and when this happens, know that the love is fading away on both sides. It means that you don't love and care about each other anymore. Such anomaly can cause tension that will turn to unexpected arguments that will lead to breakup and divorce that will leave the children with broken hearts. The best thing to do when tension arises is to walk away. By doing so, you throw water on the heat or fire that was burning in your relationship or marriage. And when partners or spouses act in such positive way, they are investing and planting good seed to nourish their relationship or marriage.

Poor communication can crush any relationship or marriage into little pieces and take away everything good and positive things they had. Never stop sharing in a romantic relationship or marriage; and the minute it happens, the care, the love, the passion, and the understanding will also vanish. When we support each other in a relationship no matter what, we kick out to the curve any problem, conflict, and argument. Also we will stay closer to one another so we can bury together all toxic communication and assaults in such relationship or marriage. Poor communication is the nightmare of most relationships or marriages that's killing them softly. It will walk all over our self-esteem and self-confidence. In a romantic relationship or marriage, it's imperative that we listen to each other with open ears because it will develop effective listening skills. That's the path to understanding and supportive relationships or marriages. I want romantic partners and spouses to understand that in a real romantic relationship or marriage, there's no winner nor loser because it's not a game, who wins, who loses. It's not and it will never be. Also it's not about me, myself, and I. It's about us, and that's the way it should be. That's why it's vital to stay focused on the other person than yourself. That's what romantic relationships or marriages are all about—compromise, understanding and mutual respect—and that's caring for one another.

Poor communication skills in a relationship or marriage is a big obstacle. Matter of fact, it is the biggest and the largest "sponsor" of conflict in these two. The effects of poor communication in a relationship or marriage are unbearable, and it will threaten the health and the happiness of both partners in such relationship or marriage. Some couples do communicate, but my question to you is, how do you communicate? You can communicate poorly or effectively. Because of poor communication, a lot of problems in relationships or marriages stayed unresolved when they could easily be solved with effective communication. That is why the divorce or breakup rate is so high around the world. As partners or spouses, we have to look and analyze what is working for us and what is not, what keeps our relationship or marriage happy and healthy so we can choose what is best for us and keep our movement going on the right path. In a dispute or argument, one of us has to stay positive and focus on what the other person is saying and try his or her best to bring solution because when we see and understand things differently, things will change for the better. And that is what positivity does. It brings change and solution. When a partner has negative attitude in a relationship or marriage, it doesn't help the other person at all. All it does is destroy what you take time to build together. The reality is if we want to grow and strive in a marriage or relationship, we must put negativity aside and adopt positivity so we can communicate more and be together forever. Positive communication is essential. It makes all the difference.

Negativity in a marriage or relationship is a poison that kills instantly; on the other hand, positivity is a lifesaver when it comes to these two components (awareness). When we find ourselves in a negative mood, we allow ourselves to be miserable, argumentative, disrespectful, critical, and defensive. With such negative attitude, we're just putting ourselves and our surroundings through hell. But when we find ourselves in a positive mood at all times, we allow ourselves to be compassionate, kind, respectful, and understandable. With such positive attitude, we bring peace and love upon ourselves and our surroundings; therefore, choose positivity for better relationships, marriages, and a stress-free life. Many romantic relationships suffer because of a lack of communication. Girlfriend and boyfriend, husband and wife refuse to bring the right seed to nourish their romantic relationships and marriages. They don't know or they just don't make the effort to understand that "communication is the key that opens all doors," as they say. No one should expect a romantic relationship to survive without the right seed to nourish it (communication). Miscommunication can bring pain and suffering in a romantic relationship. Communication comes both ways in a romantic relationship because we love and nourish each other. A romantic relationship with no communication is a mute romantic relationship, and there will be misunderstanding, and that is exactly why we get to choose carefully the kind of seed that we offer to each other in a romantic relationship to help that romantic relationship grow (not every seed is healthy). What we need to understand and accept is that romantic relationship comes with suffering, pain, heartbreak, love, and hate; and each one of them need their own seed to keep heading to their path.

Let me justify what I just said to my readers. If suffering continues in a romantic relationship or marriage, it simply means that both romantic partners and spouses are doing something wrong one way or the other. The only thing that we are doing is that we keep nourishing our romantic relationship with the seed of suffering. Be aware that every time that we treat each other in a negative way or without mindful awareness, know that we're feeding our romantic relationship or marriage with the wrong seed. If we think and act in a positive way toward each other, we will apply the real seed each time; and every time there is mindful of awareness, then only then we would be able to dive real deep in the swimming pool of our romantic relationship to find the right seed to grow our romantic relationship, instead of feeding the wrong one to it that will kill it. After swimming real deep at the bottom of the swimming pool of our romantic relationship or marriage, if we do find out the seed that we are nourishing our romantic relationship is the right one, please keep feeding it to the romantic relationship or marriage so it can keep growing. In the other end, if we find out that the seed that we are supplying our romantic relationship or marriage is not the right seed, stop immediately because it will destroy it, and we don't need such a headache.

It's about time for us to stop killing our romantic relationship and marriage by feeding them with the seed of destruction and start nourishing them with the right seed, happiness. Most romantic relationships start on the path of Romeo and Juliette, but unfortunately, many of us don't know the proper way to nourish our romantic relationship by feeding it with the right seed. So it begins to fade away until it drops dead. That is a lack of communication, and communication can bring back to life a dying romantic relationship. In order for our romantic relationship to last, all we have to do is to nourish our love, commitment, and compassion if we really want to have an awesome one. It is not the work of one person but both spouses because we all have our responsibility to drive our romantic relationship to the right path. If we keep anger, frustration, hate, and suffering guide us in our romantic relationship, well oh well, we are not going anywhere (not further than our nose.) In order for a romantic relationship to grow, we must water it with the seed of understanding, compassion, and communication because a good romantic relationship is like a pack of beautiful roses of all colors in a garden that need to be nourished with water in order to grow more beautifully. And there is no doubt in my mind, if we keep feeding the wrong seed to our relationships, the love will fade away and will never be the same again no matter how hard we try, and it will be too late.

Some people never realize something good that they have until it's too far gone. Nourishing the good seed to our romantic partners or spouses by what we say and how we say it is what all romantic relationships need to stay alive and grow. In a second, you can transform your partner and yourself by saying the right thing and by showing your true love for him/her (mindfulness in action). Name-calling and miscommunication can make a romantic relationship suffer for many years, even destroy it for good. When it comes to this point, never blame one person by pointing your finger at each other. "It's your fault." "No, it's your fault." Trust me, it's not going to take you anywhere; rather, it will drown what you have going on. The best thing to do when it gets to that level is to calm down and start looking for solutions; bring communication into your romantic relationship, and then you will reach a better outcome. When the break of a romantic relationship is loose, both partners suffer because they went down the hill together believe it or not, and that's the truth. Therefore, it doesn't really matter whose fault it is, does it? In a romantic relationship, of course, we are going to get angry and say things that we will regret later on (harsh words). We are going to say things that are destructive to each other. When we find ourselves in the mood of fear and anger, that's exactly when we swallow poison to destroy our romantic relationship with no consideration whatsoever.

Why not make an effort to keep each other happy with a big smile in our face? Most of the time, we poison each other without knowing, and that poison slowly kills our romantic partner or spouse. When we notice that our relationship is fading away, first thing to look for is "Vautoir's antidote" (understanding, compassion, and communication). With such mindful awareness, you will have the right seed so your romantic relationship can survive. With my antidote, we can give birth to respect, true love, positive thinking, and actions that can nourish our romantic relationship and help it grow and thrive (long and lasting relationship). We, as human beings, we are hungry for love which we have every right to; but when we find it, we don't even know how to generate the love that is offered to us. Often, we find a woman/man that really loves us and would do anything for us. Unfortunately, we take that love for granted and regret it later on, and it only takes a little understanding. Communication would have saved this romantic relationship if it has been put to use. The real communication is when both partners are debating one on one and mouth to mouth with understanding and compassion. "You talk, I listen. And I talk, you listen." That is good communication, instead of talking at the same time, and such strategy will also develop your listening skills. As you already know, there is no good communicator without good listening skills. Communication has no other meaning but that; that's when mindful awareness kicks in. There is nothing more delicious than having a positive conversation. Each of us, as humans, got to learn how to communicate with ourselves and others, especially our peers, in a positive way.

Long-Lasting relationships

A long-lasting relationship can be with a romantic partner, family member, a friend, a coworker, a wife, or husband, etc. The biggest problem that's killing these relationships is a "lack of communication, trust, honesty, respect, understanding, and compassion." These elements are crucial in a romantic and loving relationship. They are the key to a happier and healthier relationship. Without these components in a relationship, trust and believe no matter what kind of relationship we find ourselves into, most likely it will not work in the long term no matter what effort we put in the relationship.

Here are six keys from Vautoir's wall of good intentions to a long-lasting relationship that I'm sharing with you

- Communication

    Without communication in any relationship, it's a waste of time, and it will be a war zone. Communication can resolve any problem before it gets out of hand and will help our relationship to grow and strive. Communicate with your partner or spouse more often for a better and lasting relationship.
- Trust

    How can we love someone without trusting that person? Is that even possible? I truly believe that it's impossible because without such valuable key (trust), both partners will be doubting each other for sure.
- Honesty

    Honesty in a relationship is crucial. As we all know, "honesty is a facet of moral character. It defines our personality, dignity, integrity and truthfulness." It also involves being trustworthy, loyal, and sincere. If someone is in a relationship and he or she doesn't show honesty, know that he or she is a liar and a cheater, can't trust and can't love a liar or a cheater.

- Respect

    Respect isn't handed out to anybody. If you want respect, you have to earn it. It's imperative to respect one another in a relationship. It's a two-way street that will take us to our journey (long-lasting relationship) with no GPS needed.
- Understanding

    Understanding is the ability to understand something or someone, comprehension. When we truly understand other people, we sympathetically aware of others' feelings "pain and suffering." When we understand a partner or anyone in a relationship, that person feels secure around us, so let us show some understanding to one another for the sake of relationships.
- Compassion

    When we show compassion, we show concern for the sufferer. In a relationship, when we communicate to each other with compassion, we feel loved and protected; and no matter how high the ladder of love is, we will be able to hold hands and climb it together. Compassion is the fuel that fill the tank of a long-lasting relationship.

The biggest secret that really makes a romantic relationship works is the Word of God. "A family that prays together stays together." Most romantic relationships and marriages could have been saved, but because of a lack of the Word of God, they end up in breakup and divorce and brings a lot of stress and frustration on the children and change their lives forever. Please put the children first. They deserve it. If in a relationship your partner said or does something he or she shouldn't have done or said to you, you should talk about the situation and find some common ground together. But in a long-lasting relationship, it's not wise to hold any grudge against each other. Learn to forgive, so you also can be forgiven says the Lord.

Do what me and my wife do. We fall in love with each other every day; therefore, we leave no room for nonsense or negativity. Communicate more often. Don't try to avoid the problem or the truth. The minute we refuse to acknowledge them, they will become an issue for the relationship because they will undermine it. And when it gets to that point, it will turn your relationship upside down and shake it until it passes out, not a good thing, is it? The truth should always be told. It's better to tell the truth and face the consequences than telling a lie that will destroy your relationship. Now instead of one infraction, you will be judged for two, whatever you did, plus the lie; therefore, you are in double trouble, not wise. Then because of your negative behavior, forgiveness may not be an option, and it can also sabotage your relationship. Another thing, when telling the truth, tell it with remorse and regrets. Depending on your issue or incident, just be honest about it, and always give a sincere apology for your mistake. Be open and honest to each other, and that's a very important communication strategy. It does work, trust me. Always say thank you to your partner, along with a kiss, a hug, and an "I love you." They are good remedies to a long-lasting relationship, I promise. For such strategy to work perfectly, we need to remove all communication barriers for a healthier and happier relationship. Be aware that not every relationship is meant to be or meant for a long-term relationship. If we're really looking for a long-lasting relationship, we must be loyal, be ready to commit, and embrace the responsibility that comes with the relationship. When there's no effective communication in a relationship, both partners suffer. Taking Vautoir's antidote is a way to heal from miscommunication, misunderstanding, and disrespect in a relationship. By taking such dose, you will be able to communicate clearly and effectively. Your heart will be sinking with true love, compassion, and understanding so you can reach out to a long-lasting relationship that will put a smile on everybody's face, sweet.

Compassionate Communication in Relationships and Marriages

When you are using my antidote with your loved ones, you will see and understand that you are working to build a real family together. With compassionate communication, we can help one another to understand true love and come to our senses. We will learn to speak *mindfully* by thinking through what we are going to say. It's crucial that we listen to ourselves in a relationship or marriage. More importantly, ask yourselves some valuable questions which is the base of all successful relationships or marriages. When it comes to compassionate communication in these two components, it requires both partners and spouses to make a sacrifice to understand the need of each other. When both partners and spouses act in such positive manner, together they will be able to build a very strong and healthy relationship or marriage based on true love. Communication is one of the most important areas in relationships and marriages. It's an awesome thing, even a blessing, to have the ability to communicate compassionately. It shows an extreme desire that someone may have to understood deeply the suffering of the other person or the speaker. It's the foundation upon which any solid relationships and marriages are built. When talking or communicating compassionately, other people want to listen to you and want to trust you. Should any argument arise between your two partners or spouses, go quickly and knock on the door of compassionate communication for help so it can open its door to you in order to find a suitable resolution to the problem. Compassionate communication is not something that anybody should play with. It contains real solution for any kind of issues in a relationship or marriage. Therefore, let us communicate compassionately to our partners, spouses, and people around us so we can live as examples for others.

Happy Marriages and Relationships

Relationships and marriages nowadays are very hard to stay committed. But if each partner work hard enough to keep their relationship going or try hard to save it, it can happen because "where there's a will, there's a way." I know how hard it is to satisfy each other all the time. We're never satisfied as human beings. It's in our DNA. We can always try our best to bring happiness to one another if we really love each other the way we should; love conquers anything. Let us not forget *communication* because without this important key, the door of happiness or healthy relationship will stay locked forever, and that's the only key that can open this door. By opening the door of happiness, you will stay happy and committed as a couple, guaranteed. When there's a lack of communication in a relationship or marriage, both partners suffer.

If anyone is in one of them and want their relationship or marriage to be successful and both partners to be very happy, the first thing to do is learn how to communicate or how to express yourselves. By doing so, you will also learn how to express your worries and concerns. That is effective communication which is the big brother of happiness. Be aware that without effective communication in a relationship or marriage, happiness won't be present. And with the absence of such key element, you will end up in divorce or breakup because you are going to push away one another knowingly or unknowingly, and that's the end of that relationship or marriage. Communication is essential in a relationship or marriage. It will keep it running until it gets to its destination which is to its little brother, happiness. Do yourselves a favor, stay away from the social media. STOP texting your husband, wife, girlfriend, boyfriend, etc., on important and private subjects. The most intelligent way to discuss your issues, concerns, and worries is one on one. Such strategy will eliminate confusion, misunderstanding, arguments, violent language, and it will STOP us from jumping to conclusions because our good intention or what we meant to express might be seen or understood differently by our partner or spouse. And we will keep all other people out of our business or personal life (nosy people). If you and your lover can't meet right away and you feel as though you have to discuss the matter right away, give him or her a ring. It's way match better to discuss the matter over the phone. "Let us talk." If you do just that, I guarantee you that the quality of your relationship or marriage will improve 100 percent. When you improve your communication skills, your relationship or marriage smiles; but when your communication skills is absent or nonexistent, then your marriage or relationship cries because it's sad and unhappy.

Be truthful in your marriage or relationship and be a man or woman of your word by letting your word become your bond. Integrity in a marriage or relationship tells a lot on both partners and spouses. When you promise something, do it. Don't break your promise; if you say that you are going to do something, do it for the sake of your integrity, marriage, or relationship.

The minute you broke your promise or you don't do what you said you were going to do, know that your partner or spouse starts having doubts about you and starts seeing you for what you are not and will never be and starts losing faith in you. Such feeling will force to give your partner or spouse a ride and drop him or her to the unhappy mood zone that will create, sooner or later, what you call "conflict." Believe it or not, your partner or spouse will stop trusting and believing in you; therefore, be careful so your partner or spouse doesn't see in you a liar. Keep the happiness going by keeping your promise and your word for the 2022 by making a drastic change to save your marriage or relationship so both of you can stay happy and healthy.

Communication is not only the key that opens the door of all relationships or marriage, but it's also the starter that allows your marriage or relationship to start and take the right direction to its destination. When I talk about relationship, I don't stay focus only on intimate relationships, and that is why I said all relationships. It can be friendship, coworker relationship, and family member relationship, etc., in this world that God has created. We have all kinds of people in it. We see, think, and understand things differently.

For example, if we have fifty people in the same situation, each one will react differently toward the situation. Why is that? Well, because we think and act differently from one another. Also, it is impossible to know what our partner is thinking because we can't read minds, and that is why we have to communicate with each other so we can be on the same page. Let the vibes of communication do its way in our marriage or relationship for the sake of a good and prosperous marriage or relationship. And most importantly, open our hearts to God if we really want to be happy because the best happiness that we can get from our marriage or relationship comes from God. Know that he loves us. And he wants to help us, and he is the only one that will not betray us and can better our lives and bring joy and happiness into our marriage and relationship; he got his eyes on us.

Healthy Marriages and Relationships

In a marriage or relationship, we see love, respect, intimacy, compassion, understanding, good communication skills, and most importantly, a sense of value from both partners because both of these elements are two-way streets, not one way. And when both partners and spouses see it and understand it this way, they will automatically become a healthy marriage or relationship, one that is valued by both partners and spouses. A healthy marriage or relationship keeps both partners or spouses happy and smile at all times, but on the other hand, an unhappy marriage or relationship brings the contrary, which I will talk about later. It's always good and smart to dig real deep in the basket of marriage and relationship on a day-to-day basis to come up or to create healthy marriage and relationship that will become the relationship (health insurance) of both spouses and partners (health for life). It is true that most of us heard or talked about healthy relationships or healthy marriage, without having a clue how to get or build one because we have no training in that sort. Guess what, it is never too late to learn. We can still learn and share with others by communicating more to one another. And when we communicate to each other, we will learn from one another, and that's what communication is all about.

In a healthy marriage or relationship, we have to learn to get rid of every habit or everything that can turn our healthy marriage or relationship into an unhealthy one.

Here are three key elements that can keep our marriage or relationship happy.

- Self-awareness

    Self-awareness is about understanding. Be alert and in sight. When we are aware of things, we place ourselves in the "know zone." We will automatically know our needs, wants, why we do what we do, why we say what we say, why we act the way we act and the repercussions, etc. And we will have a better idea of who we really are. Let's say, for example, that we are having a conversation or communicating with our partner or spouse. We will know what to say and what not to say (self-awareness). That's very healthy, don't you think? Being aware is having the ability to anticipate our positive or negative consequences of our thoughts, behaviors, feelings, and actions. Therefore, self-awareness teaches us how to manage our attitudes, behaviors, how to think and react to any situation so we can make the right decision and stay healthy.

- Mutual respect

    Mutual respect is be respectful, to be respected. Both partners have valuable and very important contributions to make in a relationship or marriage in order to keep it healthy. When partners or spouses demonstrate mutual respect in a marriage or relationship, they don't only show they care for each other but also for themselves. Such door should never be closed. It should stay open at all times to welcome healthy marriage and relationship.

- Compassionate love

    Compassionate love is about caring, kindness, and willingness. Showing these three components in our marriage or relationship is showing our spouse and partner that we are a thoughtful and decent person, and we are aware of their pain and suffering. We understand the situation that they are going through, and we will use compassion to make things better. It is all about healthy relationship, marriage, and true love.

Marriage or relationship is a challenge, can't give up or quit. We have to give the best that we got in order to save them and stay healthy for the sake of love. In a relationship or marriage, both partners and spouses have to value communication so they don't feel rejected or unwanted. When communication is dead, each one of you is going to have negative feelings toward one another by the way which is normal.

Communication is an element that should never be taken for granted. Unfortunately most of us in a relationship or marriage do take it for granted. Mistakes are inevitable because we are just humans, and we have differences. And that's why in a relationship or marriage, communication is essential. It can fix almost any anomaly not to say all and bring peace of mind in a relationship or marriage. No relationship or marriage can grow and strive without effective communication. All of us want to be in happy and healthy marriages or relationships, and all we have to do is communicate with one another. It will also bring partners and spouses closer to each other than staying away or distancing themselves from each other. It goes both ways because it takes two to the tango. Always pay attention to each other's interest and feed into it for healthier marriage and relationship. Both partners and spouses have to bring something positive into the relationship or marriage in order to keep it happy and healthy.

Know who we are, what we want, and where we want to go with our marriage or relationship (self-awareness). This is the first thing to know when we are in a relationship, and before we get married, we have to know our values and our goal. We cannot rush to be in a relationship or marriage, lacking of any of these components. Trust me, it won't work. We need to learn to love our partner or our spouse for who they are. We can't change people, but we can only communicate with them and accept them for who they are. There's a saying in Creole, which is my language, that says, "You can force a donkey to cross a river, but you cannot force it to drink water." It means only the donkey will know if it wants to drink or not because only it knows if it's thirsty or not. So the lesson to learn here is that you can't force anyone to change. Only that person will know if he wants to change or not, "love me for who I am." Learn to accept yourself for who you really are, then only then you will accept other people for who they are. When putting yourself in such state of mind, you will accept and support your partner or your spouse no matter what. That is real love in a healthy relationship or marriage. No one can be in a healthy relationship or marriage, not knowing the true meaning of love. It's totally impossible.

For most of us, especially the new generation, think that love is based on how the person looks, and how much money or assets he or she has. That's exactly why relationships and marriages nowadays don't last, and the children are suffering the way they are suffering. The lacking of the new generation is that they don't know "love is a choice that's based on logic and reason," says the experts. We make a choice to love someone no matter what, "for better for worse," and that's what long-term relationship or marriage is all about—love. "Good times and bad times, until death do us part." Love is affection that we have for somebody. It's also a mental state where we position our deepest feeling and affection for that person that we care about, someone we want to do and share things with, have pleasure with, build with, succeed with, and have kids with. Love brings people together. It's a close bond that comes with partnership, compassion, understanding, respect, loyalty, and trust. Love is a togetherness in a relationship or marriage. It's a journey hand in hand, and that's exactly what you call "forever love."

Unhappy Marriages and Relationships

As we all know, the word *unhappy* means not pleased or satisfied with a situation or someone. Well, if we are in a marriage or relationship and we are not pleased or satisfied, it also means that we are not happy. Everybody likes to be happy. Why choose otherwise? There is nothing in this world that's more painful than staying in a marriage or relationship that we are not happy. Some people choose to stay because in their mind, they think they can make it work (meaning they can make it the way they want it to be instead of seeing it for what it is). Sometimes you can do your best to bring change or try to help your partner or spouse to see clearly, but it's just a waste of time and energy because if something is not meant to be, it's not meant to be. And there's nothing we can do about it no matter what we try and do. It's true that some of us are blinded by our love, but there's a time that we have to let go for our own sake, well-being, happiness, and health. The reality is that anyone can be in an unhappy marriage or relationship. Maybe you are in one now or have been in one in the past and don't want to face that situation or be in that same nightmare again; it's understandable.

If you feel unhappy in a marriage or relationship because things are not the way you expect them to be, here are some steps that you should take.

- Unhappy

    First you have to determine are you really unhappy with your marriage or relationship, or the problem is just you unhappy with yourself. You have to be able to make that valuable distinction before you can decide if to stay or to move on. Stress and frustration in the past or from life itself can easily infiltrate in your awesome marriage or relationship that you are having with the love of your life and turn it into a nightmare. Most people that are married or in a relationship always carry home with them all the problems that they encounter doing the day and take it on their partner or spouse who has nothing to do with it which, by the way, is very unfair. For example, let's say that we have a rough day at work, and we have a lot of work to do and to return to our boss at a certain day and time. Unfortunately we didn't finish the job on time, and the boss has decided to keep us for four more hours to finish the job without pay. Of course, we are not going to be happy about it, who would? But it is what it is. The problem is when we got home, the minute we go to the door, we start taking it on our partner or spouse; what does he or she have to do with anything? If we use our common sense the way we should, it would tell us that they don't have anything to do with what happened. We're just being irresponsible, logically. All we have to do is take responsibility for our own action or mistake and work harder to better the situation.

- Differences/conflicts

    All marriages and relationships have their ups and downs, and there is no perfect marriage or relationship. We have our differences, and we take them with us wherever we go, plus no one is perfect. Therefore, conflicts do and will always happen between partners and spouses but, most importantly, is not to look at the conflict itself but learn how to resolve the problem by communicating your way through it with compassion, respect, and lots of understanding for great results and healing (Vautoir's antidote).

- Time to let go

    If we feel that the marriage or the relationship is really the one that's causing us to be unhappy and turning our lives upside down, then it's time to get out as quick as possible without thinking about the time, energy, and money already invested in that marriage or relationship. It's worth it to let go, especially if you don't have children together, and start a new life than regret it later on. We must think about our health and happiness because everybody deserves to be healthy and happy. If the marriage or relationship is not helping us to grow and strive in any way, there is no need to stay.

I know it can be hard, but at the same time, we cannot be stuck at something that's making our lives miserable, unhappy, and unhealthy. We have to do what is best for us because we are the only one who can really take good care of us.

Life is good and sweet, brothers and sisters. Don't let nobody or anything take this flavor away from your mouth. You have every right in the world to enjoy every second, every minute, every hour, and every day the sweetness, the goodies, the healthy and happy moments of life. It is a God-given right that no man can take away from you no matter what. It is your life and your health; therefore, take good care of them. Please stay happy and healthy.

Wisdom in Marriages and Relationships

"Wisdom is having knowledge and good judgement, it is also the quality of being smart, principles." To have wisdom in a marriage or relationship is not that hard like it seems. All we need is self-awareness, be aware of our partner or spouse. Know that we are not alone, and we are a team. So we have an obligation to treat our partner or our spouse like we would like to be treated. Talk to him or her the way we would want to be talked to. Remember our partner or spouse has feelings too; therefore, their feelings can be hurt the same way yours can. Having wisdom in a marriage or relationship is nourishing them with the right seed and watering them with the right love so we can live happily ever after.

Here are three ways that we can acquire wisdom!

Firstly, wisdom in a marriage or relationship is not something that any partner or couple should take for granted. And the best way to gain knowledge when it comes to wisdom is to pray and read the Word of God so we can be blessed and stay blessed. And so we can strive for success and greatness and bring peace upon ourselves and our surroundings. When a couple prays together, read the Word of God together, they are walking together to meet with the wisdom of our creator and savior, Jesus Christ.

Secondly, the second way we can acquire wisdom is from our past experience using our mistakes. By giving our past a phone call, we will see what went wrong, not who's right, who's wrong, just the cause or the source of the problem. I know sometimes it's painful to go back, but it will give us some wisdom not to make or repeat the same mistake again and start nourishing our new relationship or marriage with some good seed so we can keep moving to the right direction toward happiness and true love.

Thirdly, an excellent way of gaining knowledge and wisdom besides of the two ways above is to read books and watch videos on marriages and relationships. There are some good books out there written by some experts on romantic relationships.

Forgiveness in Relationships and Marriages

When you forgive someone for doing you wrong, it's when you put all negative thinking and feelings behind you and start over, when you stop feeling angry toward that person who offended you or just made a simple mistake. What does God say about forgiveness?

In Mark 11:25, "Be kind to one another, tenderhearted, forgiving one another, as God in Christ forgave you. And whenever you stand praying, forgive if you have anything against anyone, so that your father who is in heaven may forgive you your trespasses."

Research has revealed that a lack of forgiveness stirs up negative emotions and creates more conflicts. Brothers and sisters, forgiveness is the ladder to any happy and healthy marriage or relationship. Anyone in a relationship or marriage should know that if they practice forgiveness, it will drop them right on the path of a long-lasting relationship or marriage.

Forgiveness is the golden key that opens the door of a happy and healthy marriage or relationship simply because nobody is perfect, and the word *mistake* is in our blood. We were born with it, and we're going to die with it. There's no other way.

I choose to forgive for four reasons:

- Because God says so
- Because I want also to be forgiven
- Because I am not perfect, and I do make mistakes just like everybody else
- Because of our differences

As humans, we are all different from one another, by the way we think and act; therefore, disappointment is inevitable. It is in everyone's best interest to understand, respect, and accept as people that we have different minds and see and understand things differently.

Each and every one of us, as human being, has feelings, emotions, and anger; one way or the other, we are subject to make mistakes. But such awareness doesn't give any green light to any one of us to abuse others in anyway or sit back, let some people walk all over us. However, in reality, if we want to grow and strive in a long-term relationship or marriage with a partner or a spouse that we love and value and we want to spend the rest of our life with, we should learn how to forgive; it's a must. When we choose not to forgive, we also choose not to solve the conflict or the problems that are tearing up the net of our relationship or marriage.

No matter how hard we try to save our relationship or marriage, without forgiveness, it is a waste of time. No matter what we do, conflict will always be there—can't stop it, can't chase it away. It is up to us as partners or couples to find a way to live quietly and peacefully around it, and the best way to do that is to walk slowly hand in hand with forgiveness. When we don't forgive, we choose to light up the fire under the pot of our relationship or marriage knowingly or unknowingly so we can warm up the negative feelings, emotions, and create much more conflict and that is not healthy for neither one of us as partners or couples. It is imperative that we learn how to compromise so we can easily open the door of forgiveness, and resolve problems within our relationship or marriage. Forgiveness is the "antifreeze" that keeps the radiator and the engine of our relationship or marriage going, and without it, they will run hot. When we practice forgiveness as partners or couples, we automatically control our behaviors and have positive attitudes toward each other (no resentment and no grudge). It's a blessing when you see in a relationship or marriage the two people put great effort to forgive, and to maintain a positive attitude in which they love and cherish one another, most importantly with no hostility. But when we refuse as partners or couples to practice forgiveness, one way or the other, we will pay the repercussion, which are the followings:

- It will bring anger, hate, frustration, grudge, conflict, and arguments into the relationship or marriage.
- It will bring stress, depression into our lives.

- It will create an inability to enjoy or stay connected to one another.
- Both of us will feel a lack of purpose and happiness.

When we fail to forgive others, we also fail to forgive ourselves. Forgiving our partner, wife, husband, friend, coworker, or a family member when they make a mistake can be very hard. When we feel betrayed and angry, it is not easy at all to forgive. We always look for a way to hurt back the person who hurt or upset us (revenge). Trying to change such feeling can be very difficult and might take some time, but still we have to do our best to forgive. It is very important; it is one of God's laws. "Forgive but do not forget." When we forgive another person, we are walking in the right direction to meet with communication that will lead us to happiness by leaving behind all negativity and transgressions so we can succeed together. That is also another way to be kind to ourselves so we can protect ourselves from drinking poison such as stress, frustration, resentment, anger, hate, anxiety, and grudge; they are killers. Why in the world that somebody would want to poison himself or herself over someone's mistake or stupidity? Makes no sense, right? When we forgive the person who does us wrong, we establish or build our own barrier to block all negative feelings that can hunt us down so we can be poison free. And I know some people might say, well, if we forgive the offender, we will become vulnerable. It is like opening our door to them so they can hurt us more. Not really, most offenders will play on the second chance that they got so they can make things better, not to make them worse and know that everybody deserves a second chance. If they mess up again, we have all the right in the world to kick them out of the curve.

In a relationship or marriage, it is vital that we always look for a way to communicate and try our best to understand the other person. The real solution is in communication, not confrontation. Communication will lead to solution, but confrontation will bring more conflict. And more conflict will bring all other negative things that we can think about. Let us forgive each other so we can find the right seed to feed our togetherness. May the law of forgiveness play its part in every relationship and marriage around the world so more happiness can take place in the families. May the good will of our Lord guide us all.

Obedience in Marriages and Relationships

Obedience is the roots of all successful marriages and relationships. Obedience and intimacy are unbreakable and inseparable, and they are both essential for a growing and striving relationship or marriage. If we are not obedient to one another, ultimately intimacy is nonexistent. Therefore, we are subject to downfall, deception, cheating, lies, conflict, arguments, and the pitfalls of sin which would make the devil very happy because that is where he takes pleasure, and that is what he likes. He would like to see that every child of God falls into his pit of sin so their souls can be his.

The devil has nothing good and positive in him. He's just a liar and a deceiver. Obedience only comes from God. In order to be obedient, we have to acknowledge God first; and by acknowledging him, we will be able to acknowledge and obey our partner, spouse, and others. God our creator put marriage as a commitment between a man and a woman, and each have for duty to submit to him and one another.

In the beginning of time, as we all know, God made man (Adam) from dust and breathed life into him and became human. Then God, in his good judgement, found out that it wouldn't be appropriate for the man to live alone; and in this context, he created Eve for Adam by taking a rib from Adam and made the love of his life. And when God brought her to Adam, he was very happy and joyful, and he was not ashamed to praise Eve. Adam said, "This is now bone of my bones and flesh of my flesh; she shall be called "woman," for she was taken out of man" (Genesis 2:23, NIV).

Everything was working accordingly to God's plan, and peace was among them while obeying the Word of God, and they were content of one another. But the devil came and scattered the seeds of unbelief, greediness, and disobedience in their mind to the Word of

God. And when God asked Adam the reason for his disobedience, he accused Eve, the woman. Sin entered their marriage life through disobedience (Genesis 3:1–12).

The tactic that the devil used is very simple. He makes sure that Adam and Eve loses focus on what God told them to do and God's intention when it comes to marriage so the devil have "shifted" their focus. But if we take a minute and look at marriages around the world today, we could say that the same tactics are still being used by the devil to destroy families and change the real meaning of marriage. As human beings, our duty is to always seek God's Word and his will so we can bring blessings upon us, especially our children.

When we obey the Word of God, we're not just being obedient, but also we're building a solid wall of protection around our families that no earthquake can destroy. As humans, we all dream to be loved and have the ideal marriage. The only way we can do that is to put God first in everything that we do. Then we will be able to resist the devil and his evil tactics.

Ephesians 5:22–33 (KJV) said,

- "Wives, submit yourselves unto your husbands as unto the Lord."
- "For the husband is the head of the wife, even as Christ is the head of the church: and he is the savior of the body."
- "Therefore, as the church is subject unto Christ so let the wives be to their own husbands in everything."
- "Husbands, love your wives, even as Christ also loved the church, and gave himself for it."
- "That he might sanctify and cleanse it with the washing of water by the word."
- "That he might present it to himself a glorious church, not having spot, or wrinkle, or any such thing; but it should be holy and without blemish."
- "So aught man to love their wives as their own bodies. He that loveth his wife loveth himself."
- "For no man ever yet hated his own flesh, but nourisheth and sherisheth it, even as the Lord the church."

- "For we are members of his body, of his flesh, and of his bones."
- "For this cause shall a man leave his father and mother, and shall be joined unto his wife, and they two shall be one flesh."
- "This is a great mistery: but I speak concerning Christ and the church."
- "Nevertheless, let everyone of you in particular so love his wife even as himself, and the wife see that she reverence her husband."

The biggest anomaly or challenge that marriage is facing today is a "lack" of the Word of God or a total misinterpretation of the Word of God. The word *submit* is misinterpreted by many men around the world. God says, "Wives submit to your husbands." Many men took the word *submit* out of context by thinking that the word means for their wives to become their slaves or servants. The word *submit* doesn't mean to become a slave or a servant. It just simply means that the wives have a mission and to be under such mission. Therefore, the real meaning of the phrase "wives submit to your husbands means wives be under the mission of your husband the same way that the husbands are under the mission of God," is to love, cherish, protect, and nourish their wives. The Word of God doesn't say for a man to dominate his wife to treat her like an object or to show that husbands are superior or better than their wives. And I also don't see in the Bible, not once, where it stated that men have more power over women; therefore, they have to dominate women.

The Bible only teaches us men how to treat and love our women with kindness, compassion, understanding, tenderness, respect, and gentleness because they are half of us men. This is a wonderful and awesome mission that every woman should be under just like my wife Yvonie. One thing that I am against and will always be is for a woman to put herself under the submission or mission of her abusive husband, cheating husband, or a husband that is treating her in any kind of way. My advice to you is never submit to any man that is treating you in such way; you can do better, and you deserve better.

Another thing, sisters, please STOP judging a man because of his level of education or what he has. Rather, judge him for who he really is and his belief. Only then you will be able to find yourselves some good men that will become great husbands that will keep you happy, healthy, and prosper. And never forget to put God first in everything that you do, especially in your marriage, so you can have a long-lasting marriage, "until death do us part." May the love of God be with you all.

CHAPTER 3

Parenting at Its Best

Parents vs. Children Communication

For sure, children learn how to talk and communicate by listening to their parents. The positive parents talk with respect to their kids and choose their words carefully. They know deep down that they are the role model for their children. On the other hand, you have the negative parents who use all kinds of profanity around their children and, most of the time, who even cuss at their children. And these kinds of parents wonder why their children are talking back to them and show them no respect. What these negative parents don't understand is that when they are disrespectful to their children, the children will not show them any respect either. "You reap what you sow." The words those negative parents use when talking or cussing at their children (toxic or harsh words) are like bullets or knife wounds, and they leave unforgettable and difficult to heal in-and-out scars. And as a result, the children talk to them in the same manner in the state of mind to hurt these parents the same way and to make them feel what they feel.

For those who don't know, it's a war among parents and children in the inner cities or ghettos. This war is also in the suburbs but not as terrifying as the one in the ghettos. The negative parents don't understand that they have to talk and treat their children with respect so their children can act the same way toward other people. They think because they are adults and they are the parents, they don't have to communicate with their children in a kind and respectful way. That's wrong thinking and bad parenting. Each and every parent ought to communicate with their children openly and effectively for better children and societies (positive vibes). It can be about sex, drugs, alcohol, crime, or else. Good and effective communication among parents and children will bring everyone to the bus of mutual understanding. And this bus of mutual understanding will take everybody to the final stop of mindfulness that will guide such family to one state of mind (respect). When parents communicate in a positive or effective manner with their children and place all negativity in a trash bag and dump it in the dumpster, there is a 99 percent chance that the children act the same (raising with benefit). Such "positive vibes" will not be for a short term, rather for their entire life. And they will pass it from generation to generation which will give us better communities, nations, countries, and a better world with better and respectful citizens.

Experts say, "Children begin to form ideas and beliefs about themselves based on how their parents communicate with them."

That is so true because if parents communicate with them effectively or in a positive manner at all times, it will show them that their parents have great respect for them ("positive parents, positive children," "negative parents, negative children"). It's a fact, believe it or not. When parents listen to their children with open ears (deep listening) and show them respect and understanding, they will feel as though it is power to their self-esteem that will make them think positively about themselves and can accomplish anything in life. But in the same token, when we have negative parents that are lying, cussing, yelling, and beating their children constantly for no reason at all, it automatically changes the mind-set of these children, just like changing a page of a book to go to the next one. They become violent, hardheaded, and hateful and don't value other people's life or their own, miserable parents or baby makers with no sense of how to really raise children and also with a lack of communication skills make their children feel unwanted and unimportant. Unfortunately, this is a terrible feeling that can push some children to commit suicide or hate everybody, including themselves, a situation with a possibility to turn them into criminals. Thank God that me and my wife have what it takes to raise our children the right way. Most of the time, these kinds of children with no hesitation will turn against their parents and kill them, which is very unfortunate and sad. Stress and frustration are two very dangerous weapons that can kill unexpectedly. When we communicate effectively with our children, we are teaching them how to be positive and respectful. Therefore, such children will listen to their parents and do what they're told to do. They will do it simply because they feel respected and loved, and with such feeling, they'll feel happy and joyful. And this positive feeling will grab, without a doubt, obedience. It's not magic. It's just simple math of mindfulness. And these children know very well their parents. They know what their parents are capable of doing and what they won't do, and it will raise the bar of trust on both sides. Trust and believe, children know what to expect from their parents, and parents know what to expect from their children, vice versa. Therefore, trust becomes the symbol of the family for a better family. When children know what their parents expect from them, don't you know that they will do their best to live up to these expectations? Such state of mind will give more power to the children to do the right thing and become more cooperative to their parents and siblings in the household. What we need to know and believe as parents is that the way we communicate and treat our children have a big impact on them and on us.

Such impact can bring positive vibes or negative vibes. If it's a positive conversation, it will have a positive impact on all of us, parents and children. On the other hand, if it's a negative conversation, it will have a negative impact on the children and parents. Communication has many branches. It can be effective or ineffective, positive or negative, helpful or unhelpful, the choice is ours. My bit of advice to every parent is it's imperative for parents to communicate positively, effectively, and openly with their flesh and blood. Such method will be beneficiary to each and everyone in the family, including extended families such as cousins, aunts, uncles, grandmothers, and grandfathers, etc. Not only that, such attitude will improve the relationships among them as well (talking from experience). It just brings fuel to the tank of both parents and children for a better socializing family (children first).

The best way to communicate with our children is when they're still young and also when they are not mad or angry. By doing so, we will dig real deep inside their brain to plant the goods that we are teaching them, which is the seed of righteousness. But if we, as parents, have decided not to communicate with them while they are young and wait until they turn young adults, it will be too late. They will take over, and there is nothing we will be able to do about it. They will tell us what to do and when to do it, where we can and can't go. They will control us from head to toe. It will feel like as though they have the remote control of our lives in the palm of their hands. Also it's always good for parents and children to communicate in the right state of mind or mood. All parents, by law of parenting, should make themselves available when their children need their attention. When we show our children that we really care about them and we truly want them to succeed in every corner of their life, they will leave their doors open for us as parents so we can go in and communicate with them from time to time. So when we communicate effectively with them from time to time, they feel excited, loved, and understood. Therefore, they take pleasure in sharing their thoughts, feelings, and worries with their parents with no problems or doubts. When children feel comfortable around their parents and let their doors open to them, when children can communicate with their parents with no hesitation, be aware that there is an indestructible bridge that is built so they can cross over so you can meet with each other on the other side of communication.

Positive parents are very sensitive to the words that they are using with or around their children. They know what to say and the right time to say it, and they are also aware of what not to say (mindfulness). Their mind-set tells them clearly that every word that they use is a message sent to their children that will be cached and kept. Positive message will take the children to a positive state of mind or the right mood. For example, if the father or the mother says something like, "You can come to me anytime with any question or concern that you may have, honey." The message in such positive sentence is obvious. Such parent is telling the child, "You are first in my life. Nothing is more important than you and I care about your needs" (effective communication).

For the negative parents, they see, understand, and do things differently. They always place themselves in the bad-mood zone and never pay attention to their children. A negative behavior like this one, sending a negative message to the children stating, "You are unwanted. Your needs are not my concern, and you're not important to me." Imagine what kind of impact such a negative behavior can have on these children! It will also lock all doors on effective communication and will possibly bring drama, war, violence, hate, and crime in the family, unfortunately. Why can't these negative parents have the ability to understand that there comes a time where their children need their undivided attention? Why can't they understand that it's extremely important to leave whatever they were doing and turn their attention to their children when they have a question, want to communicate with them, or simply have a concern? Is it really that difficult? What kind of message do they think that they are sending to their children? Well, the message is simple. They are telling their children that whatever they have to say doesn't matter or not important.

It's clear that sometimes parents can be extremely busy at the moment to listen to their precious children. But understand this, do it in a professional way, in a way that your children won't take offense or feel hurt. You can say something like this: "Honey, Daddy or Mommy is very or extremely busy now. Can we talk in a few when I'm done here? And you know what you have to say is very important to me." When we send a positive message like this one, such message does his homework in the mind-set of this child. He or she will understand where you are coming from and will respect your wish. They will show understanding. That's good parenting and effective communication. Compare to the negative parent that would say something like, "Don't you see that I'm busy? Get the hell out of my face or get the hell away from me." See the difference, two different people with two different methodology; one is good, and one is bad. Poor kids, they deserve better. Please be the best parents that you can be.

Listening with Open Ears in a Silent Mode

Positive parents, without a doubt, listen to their children with open ears in a silent mood. It is crucial that we don't interrupt our children while trying to communicate with us. It is a must, as parents, that we let them finish expressing their thoughts, feelings, and concerns so we can really know where they stand, where they are at, and how they feel about certain things that are going on in their lives and in the family. Listening deeply in a silent mood will automatically tell them that we care; and we also listen to them with compassion, understanding, and respect so we can communicate better. It also shows that with "Vautoir's antidote," we have no worries.

When children are talking, they want to make sure that the person or the people that they are talking to or communicate with are listening attentively. If we want to show them that we are listening to them deeply. We can open our ears widely in a silent mode without any interruption. If we cut them off without finishing their saying, we will be responsible for the breakdown of their helicopter of thoughts, and this can be very damaging.

Experts say, "In order to get children to open-up, parents should try to avoid asking questions that require only a yes or no answer. While asking the right questions can help a conversation down the road. Parents need to be careful not to ask too many questions while conversing with their children. When this happens, conversations can quickly turn into interrogation, and children will be much less likely to open up." They also say, "It is required to use open-ended questions that begin with the words 'what,' 'where,' 'whom,' or 'how' are often very useful in getting children to open up." It is also recommended that "parents use a language of love than authority when talking to their children."

Such method will keep communication alive among parents and children. When there's no positive or effective communication in a family, it causes everybody to suffer one way or the other. Therefore, "Vautoir's antidote" can kick in to heal such wounds. It will bring loving speech and keep the door of communication open to parents and children. With this kind of communication, not only they will understand each other, but everyone in the family is going to be happy and finally find the peace of mind that they were looking for. Believe me, brothers and sisters, when parents and children cross the bridge of communication and reach to the other side, they can only see joy and happiness. That's when true love emerges on the surface of the relationship simply because it's based on true understanding. Parents who know how to really listen to their children while talking are parents that learned and practiced listening skills. In every area in life, in order to do something and successfully do it, it has to be learned said the experts. Nobody can communicate effectively without good listening skills. When parents who know how to listen, listening to their children just show them that they understand what their children are saying or talking about. In the same token, the negative or bad parents will do the total opposite. They will interrupt. They will pretend that they are listening when they are not. They will show no interest in what their children are saying or talking about. It's like their children are inexistent (real bad parenting).

Positive parents know that in order to show their children that they really take interest in their concern, feelings, and worries, they know it's a must to maintain eye contact with them while talking to them about important matters or issues just to assure their children that they are here and they are listening.

Communicating Doing Arguments

As we all know, all families are argumentative at one time or another. Conflicts will rise at the highest level that we would never imagine at one point. But while such argument can be very problematic, make sure they don't turn into nightmares. There are multiple things that parents can do to prevent the argument getting to a certain level or out of hand.

Here are some techniques that I pick from my "mindfulness" just for you and your precious children:

- Smooth talk

    As parents, don't be so argumentative with your children; learn to give them the right away. In such situation, parents have to listen more and talk less. While talking, talk smoothly or softly with a calm voice in a way to capture the attention of your children. "Don't fight fire with fire," very bad idea, a destructive one. All you have to do is throw water on the fire, not adding gasoline.

- Don't try to solve all problems at once

    "Little by little the bird build its nest." When a bird is building its nest, it doesn't bring all of its materials at once. It does it little by little. It's the same for parents when arguing. It's in the family's best interest for parents to try to solve one problem at a time. It's not helpful at all to try to bring solution to all problems at the same time. But it doesn't mean, as parents, we cannot bring multiple solutions. Be flexible by trying alternative solutions. By doing so, we're teaching our children how to handle conflicts the right way (positive vibes).

- Find the easiest route to solve problems

    A problem remains a problem, but when it comes to looking for solutions, we will find multiple solutions to that problem, depending on what we are looking for. Arguments can be very disruptive. It's up to the parents to work together with their children to find suitable resolutions.

    To all parties, "effective communication," and remember, all problems have solutions; if you cannot find the solution, it's not a problem.

- Be kind and respectful

    Parents shouldn't turn their back on the rules that govern respect and kindness simply because in their state of mind, they think they can say, treat, and do whatever they pleased with their children. "It's my child." So what, does it give you the right to walk all over a human being because he or she is your child? They deserve respect too. They are humans after all, so they deserve respect just like everybody else. Even in a conflict, parents should maintain their cool so they don't say something regretful to their own children. Certain say you can't take back and can leave wounds for life. Therefore, "think before you talk."

- Listening to our children compassionately

    Good or positive parents always listen to their children compassionately, knowing that by listening to their children's perspective will allow them to discover more about their children and will also help them grow. Listening to the children compassionately will help parents to work on their listening skills also. By using compassionate listening, parents will be able to communicate 100 percent more effectively with their children (been there, done this). One huge mistake that some parents make often is that when their children are right and they are wrong, they refuse to admit it and apologize to their children. And what they don't know is that, voluntary or involuntary, they're teaching their children not to admit guilt and to be irresponsible people, and that's very scary. When you admit your guilt and you apologize for it, it makes you a better person, and people respect you for that, even those who never apologize for their mistakes to anybody. Trust and believe, the children will learn from such positive attitude.

But also let us not forget that some people hate to be challenged. It makes them nervous and uncomfortable. Believe it or not, children take pleasure in challenging their parents. They love to look for their parents' weak point so they can keep punching them in this particular spot until they give up or knock them down like a Mike Tyson punch. Only someone that listens compassionately to others talking can become an effective communicator. By listening compassionately to our children, it's like going inside their head to see what's really going on with their brain, and that's the best way ever to gather some valuable information. Parents, when we listen compassionately to our children, we build trust and a bond among parents and children. Believe me, when that trust and bond are built, they will become indestructible just like a solid rock, and it will bring respect on both sides. That's one of the master pieces in solving problems and conflicts.

By listening to them with compassion, they will learn to listen to you the same way. "You listen to me. I'll listen to you too." "You don't listen to me. Why should I?" And that's exactly how children think. You probably asking yourselves, how does he know? Well, the answer is this: I used to get inside my children mind. That's exactly how I know. When they don't listen to you, it's like talking to your shadow. No matter what you say, no one is going to listen or respond to you. It's like talking to yourself like you are crazy, very awkward situation to be in. Make sure when you are listening to your children, you listen with compassion before you can give a response. By doing so, you will assure that you have heard and understand them correctly. Such strategy will help parents to become the best parents they can be for the sake of the children, parenting at its best. Many parents are wondering what they can do to make the children listen. STOP fighting, STOP talking back to them, STOP cussing, STOP being angry all the time, STOP punching the wall, etc. What if the problem is not really the children. It's just you as parents? What if you don't have what it takes to raise your children the right way? What if you're just baby makers, not real parents? As parents, we have to have the ability to listen to the children. The real solution to this anomaly is listening compassionately to them. All you have to do as responsible parents is to cross the bridge of communication so you can find yourselves on the other side of communication. When you arrive, you will be able to listen compassionately and communicate effectively with your children.

Here what you can do to listen compassionately and communicate effectively:

- Listen carefully

    Be in the right state of mind or mood when listening to the children. Do not look elsewhere when talking to them; "look them straight in the eyes." When your attention is called for as parents, give it with no hesitation by putting everything else in your pockets. Know that your children come first, and they got the power.

- Listen mindfully

    It's extremely important as parents to listen to the children with an open mind (mindfulness) than a close mind. We listen with an open mind when we listen first without interruption. Then only then we can bring our judgement, instead of not listening to them at all and assuming that we already know what they are going to say or talk about (very bad perception that will pull the children away from us parents). Now I don't think any of us would want something like that, do we? Let them speak their heart out for better communication and understanding.

- Do not interrupt

    Interrupting means listening to the children with a close mind and close ears. No child likes to be cut off like an electric switch light where we think, as parents, we have the right to finish what they're saying for them. Trust me, you don't have that right because they didn't give it to you. They have the right to take a minute to think, but it doesn't give you the right to jump in. They're just taking a break so they can dig deeper in what they are going to express.

- Do not compare your children to anyone else

    I assure you that it's a huge mistake when some parents compare their children to other people. Such mentality is very damaging. It will put a giant red light on the path of the children that will stop them from achieving what they want to accomplish in life. "You sound just like your aunt." "You act just like your friend." That's not smart at all. It's a terrible move. Instead of making them believe they're somebody else, make them think and believe that they are unique and always tell them how smart they are. Listening to it all the time will make them believe it, and they will act smart. It will raise the bar of their self-esteem and guide them to the path of success.

As parents, if you can adopt or practice these positive components of compassionate listening that I bring to the table just for you as a gift would be awesome. These four elements that I provide you with is like blood running into your veins and can't live without it (it's that important). Practice them in your household, and you will notice a big change among you and the children, and I guarantee it. Always remember to be kind, respectful, and gentle to your children. Never STOP showing them love it will bring obedience and respect on their part. You will be amazed to see what compassionate listening can do for you and your children. It has the power to glue you together with your children. It will bring you peace of mind, and everything will be at ease (meaning it will bring parents and children closer for a better relationship). How fantastic is that?

Children loved to be heard rather than shut down like an electrical switch. Such component will bring connection, and connection will bring satisfaction and understanding. See, when you put yourselves in this kind of mind-set as parents, you feel better about yourselves and what you have accomplished. And when such good and wonderful feeling place you in the available position for your children, you will have better communication, understanding, and better relationship in a peaceful environment. Parents and children will be on the right side of compassionate listening and effective communication (the other side). This, right here, is also a part of "Vautoir's antidote." Take it and be at ease with yourselves and your children, the best family health formula ever. Parents listen compassionately to their children, and children listen compassionately to their parents, vice versa. That is nothing else but magic. Both parties will walk around with a magic stick called compassionate listening.

Parents vs. Children
Lack of Communication

A family with no effective or healthy communication is like driving a nice and expensive car down a hill with no brakes. It will be dangerously out of control no matter how good of a driver you are or how hard you would try to gain control. In order to avoid a child out of control, behaviors and stinky attitudes, it's vital that we bring down all barriers of communication. When we use such strategy, it will nourish and water the right seed to communication by making sure both parents and children are valued, heard, and understood. The lack of communication in a family can manifest in so many different ways. For example, a child may be having sex, stealing, lying, or becomes a gang member and nobody in the family knows about it because of a lack of communication (meaning communication is dead in such family, very dangerous situation). As parents, it's imperative to be role models for our children when it comes to healthy or effective communication. When some children see their father come home drunk every day, yelling, cussing, beating Mom, arguing all the time about every little thing and never have time for one another and not once try to support each other in anyway, therefore, without a doubt, the children will behave the same way in their relationships, with their friends, and toward each other, and that's a very ugly picture. These negative parents or baby makers never take time to sit with their children and have a decent conversation with them like they should as parents. When parents take time to communicate effectively or have healthy communication with their children, it helps them grow in a positive way and have the desire to achieve greatness and become better people and students.

Poor communication can destroy a family like a broken glass and can't put back together because, in reality, we can't do anything with a broken glass, especially if it's broken into little tiny pieces. The real key component in a successful family is healthy communication. Without this important and valuable key, as parents, we will be caught in the rain outside; and no matter how hard we will knock on the door, nobody will be home to let us in. It's like putting our two feet in one shoe, not a good and clever idea. When, in a family, everyone is screaming, cussing at each other, and arguing instead of communicate, using violence, accusing, keeping secrets, using threats and hurting each other one way or the other, that's poor family communication. You can call it what you want, but it is what it is. If any parents and children reach such level of destruction, it will be hard or almost impossible for this family to come close again (poor communication, and poor development). It's vital that, as parents, we control the way that we are communicating with our love ones because it can affect or impact their positive development in life by the way they will see themselves, interact with other people. The negative feelings and thinking can be devastating and destructive at the same time. The children will become very rebellious. They won't listen. They will become very disrespectful. The children won't obey the law and the law enforcement officials. They will take part in every crime and illegal activity and substance abuse. They will think that they are above the law (behavior problems). It's very easy for children who are mistreated by parents and society to develop anxiety, stress, and depression that will give them a ride and drop them in the world of bad behaviors.

It's imperative that, as parents, we put them first, treat them with respect, show them lots of love, and communicate with them on a regular basis; that's protecting our children, at the same time turning them into positive people. And by having such positive attitude, as parents, we're just erasing arguments and violence on the family's board while forming better children for better societies and a better world. Also, we will have better connection with them that will make them happy and joyful. Always give them those hugs and kisses from time to time as parents, and make sure you don't miss out on this one. It will show our children how we appreciate, love, and care about them. And that's exactly how we are going to earn our respect, love, and obedience from them. Believe me when I tell you, "I've been there, and done this." Don't minimize their feelings or say they're just children, "big mistake." We don't want to push our own children away from us. We want to be closer to them. If such mistake is made, it will be very difficult to communicate with them; and with no communication, there's no family. The only thing that will leave for such family is war in every corner of the house, not a good thing, is it? Effective or healthy communication build strong families. It's like digging real deep the foundation to build the solid wall of communication so no "earthquake" can destroy. We as parents should be able to know that society, media, and technology have a negative effect on communication. We need more face-to-face interaction in our relationships with our kids.

Online Communication

Parents, be aware that social media and technology have negative effects on our children's communication skills. Therefore, we need more face-to-face interaction in our relationships with them. Look how addicted or obsess that children of this generation are to their phone when it comes to games, text, social media, etc. This monster called "technology" is robbing our children from socializing with people; in other words, it's robbing them from the ability to communicate with others through their relationships, friendships, etc. They are also losing the interest or the desire to listen to others talking or communicating with them. Most of them have no skills whatsoever when it comes to communication, and I don't have to be a genius to figure that one out neither. The facts are there.

Here are four communication skills that children these days are missing and that need a serious intervention.

- The ability to help others

    When children spend excessive amount of time on their phone, they don't think of others at all. That's the reason why they never put themselves in the position to serve others that are in need. It can be a friend, a family member, or a complete stranger. Due to a lack of time, busy on their phone, serving others is not an option or important. Some serious changes need to be done now, parents.
- Face-to-face communication

    Face-to-face communication is a process that will give children the ability to think before they talk and also will allow or require them to think and communicate spontaneously. Believe me when I tell you, device communication will destroy our children's talent to communicate effectively, but one on one communication will boost or raise the bar of their communication skills. Children nowadays feel awkward when it comes to a one on one communication simply because they don't know how to think "Every problem has a solution."

- The ability to listen deeply

    Children of this generation show great interest to listen to music, be on social media, play video games, texting or else than trying to develop the ability to listen deeply to their parents, friends, family members, or strangers when talking to. Therefore, they lack the ability to communicate effectively. The children need to engage more in communication so they can develop effective communication skills, and that's a must.

- Holding a conversation

    When children only know how to communicate through technology, how in the world will they be able to hold a decent conversation and build an argument? They won't have the ability to do so because of the lack of communication that they have. This lack is holding them back from being able to put together, as a puzzle, deeper thoughts so they could give birth to new arguments, at the same time build a solid case when it comes to communication.

Why We Should Listen to Our Children

Listening to our children as parents is vital. If we really want them to listen to us, we have to listen to them first. By listening to them, we're sending them a direct message (the importance of listening). Make sure that we create valuable time for them. They need that. Busy parents have a tendency of pushing their children away from them which send those kids a negative signal (listening to you is not important).

My advice to all parents when it comes to listening to their children:

- Take to heart your children's worries or concerns. It will encourage effective communication where both parents and children will communicate more and better their relationships. And remember communication is a two-way street.
- Parents, always show your children that you take great interest in what they have to say.
- Make sure that they have no fear to discuss important issues with you and assure them that you are not going to blame them for anything. Rather, help them to ease their fear, pain, and suffering and regrets.
- At this point, only what they have to say is important or matters, nothing else.
- Don't be judgmental so they can come back to you with other issues. By not judging, you will leave your communication door open to them.

Technology vs. Parents and Children

Technology and parents are worst enemies. It's like putting lemon in milk. Children have a better relationship with technology than their parents and the society that they're living in. Such anomaly contributes to a growing divided parents and children that will also give us divisive societies in a divided world. This divide is spread out due to the increased use of technology among our children that STOPS them from communicating with themselves, friends, and parents because they give first priority to their phones which limit their availability to have a decent conversation with their surroundings, especially their parents. It's very sad because most parents don't understand what's going on and lose the power to regulate the phone use in the house; therefore, feeling trap with their two feet in one shoe, they keep their distance in the technological lives of their children. And those who try very hard to regulate their children's use of technology didn't really bring any solution to the problem due to their children's lack of respect for their parents' authority.

This independence providing by mobile technology and computer to the children around the world is devastating and very destructive. It's a hazardous material to the health and education of the children who are using them wrongly. The absence of the house phone represent a real danger for the well-being of the children around the globe. I do remember when I used to call my girlfriend on the house phone who became my wife for eighteen years now. The phone calls most of the time were answered by her mother or her father who immediately knew who was calling and who their daughter was talking to. So these parents had the chance to control and monitor their daughter's social life (who she interacts with). Well, not any more, thanks to mobile devices or the dream killer. Things have changed. New technology has served children independence on a silver platter without their parents' involvement or consent in their social lives, especially the kind of friends they are making, the use of mobile phones, and social networking sites. This new generation see the new technology as a victory or as freedom from kicking their parents out of the curve of their personal life.

On the other side of the token, parents see it as a loss of connection to their children; and unfortunately, they feel hopeless or powerless. Families now are unable to stay connected and communicate with one another. I strongly believe that technology is taking over. It takes all the time that families use to possess due to the multiple forms of technology they have on the market such as computers, TVs, iPhone, iPods, etc., are keeping both parents and children away from each other in the modern world. This family division is the "knight" in all families' chess game, which represent a nightmare for the families, societies, and the world. These destructive devices are making sure that the freedom and the independence of the children around the world is served hot and spicy to them at a very early age, sad isn't it? Most parents have no clue who their children are interacting with every day in social media, and the children are not aware how they are putting their lives in danger. They get abducted and killed by talking and meeting with complete strangers and lie to their parents so they can meet with them. Those parents lose track of their children, not only because of a lack of communication but also because of technology that's forcing the children to lie, to cheat, to have sex, to steal, and to become gang members, etc. They don't even know their own children unless somebody tells them something they should have known about them.

Communication between parents and children is the real key that can open any door that was locked for years in any family's relationship. When a family gives priority to communication, everyone communicates, everybody will understand the needs and the wants of everybody in the family. Therefore, the relationship in such family will grow and strive. When we don't communicate with our children, they will find others to communicate with and the teaching or the conversation that they will have with them such as friends, romantic partners, family members, and strangers can be very destructive— better to talk to them as parents than other people. "Parents are the best teachers ever." Parents, please know that children take great pleasure in their independence to distance themselves from you. You and only you as parents have the power to flip the table of communication so you can better things between you and your children. Children hate to be told what to do and to be disciplined, but know that you must do it for better children. Therefore, any little chance they get, they will distance themselves from their parents, and that's exactly why they welcome technology with open arms. They love it so much. They hug the technology so tight and refuse to let go. They sleep with it. They wake up with it. And they play with it, eat with it, and go to school with it. This dangerous tool, technology, is destroying our children softly and surely, no conversation at the table, in the car, etc. Communication is dead between parents and children, and both of them are just waiting for the right moment so they can bury it together. That's deep, isn't it?

More time is needed to be spent with our children so we can teach them, play with them, communicate with them, interact with them, discipline them, and so forth. But unfortunately for most families, the technology, which I give a nickname to "techno-defect," especially the cell phone, is creeping like a ghost into parents and children's interactions, impacting parent-children relationships. For example, more than half of adults around the world are online just like the children doing their thing on a day-to-day basis (meaning the use of the cell phone is increasing every single day by parents). Therefore, there should be a big concern about the possibility of devastating repercussions that such negative behavior might have on the development and communication with the children in the family. The interaction between both parents and children is essential and crucial. Anything that disrupts the beauty, the importance, the value, the understanding, the relationship, the passion, and the love of that interaction will have a negative impact on both parents and children (very sorrowful situation). Parents, it doesn't matter where we are located around the world. We are still parents; and it doesn't change the interaction, the relationship, and the form of communication that we should have with our children because every child counts. And children are children, and they find themselves in the same basket when it comes to these important elements in life. They need our quality time and attention that will give birth to human interaction that our children are seeking for and need so desperately. The bond between parents and children around the world is fading away at a very high speed. When children are not checking their devices, their parents are and vice versa. And when there is no interaction nor communication between parents and children, there is a possibility that the children feel rejected, unwanted, and unimportant; it's a very critical situation. Technology becomes families' nightmare in almost every existing family, believe it or not.

Children are copycats. They will do what they see and repeat what they hear. Therefore, parents let us be the role models we need to be for the sake of our children. The outcomes are devastating and scary. Time to wake up; otherwise, it will be too late.

The truth is that some adults and some children nowadays unfortunately become phone and computer zombies. They are walking on the street head down to their phones like walking "zombies," bumping into other people and objects on the road or wherever they might be. They even get hit by cars because when they are crossing the street, they forget their lives and remember only their phone. And when they get home, nothing changes because they spend the rest of the day on their phone or their computer and forget about everything and everyone else. These kinds of people are developing what experts called "antisocial and addicted behavior," and they really need help. The worst thing for me is when they think nothing is wrong with them, and they are not addicted to their computer or their phone when they really are. As we all know, unfortunately, this is the age of technology. Most children nowadays have an iPhone, an iPod, etc.; but as parents, do we take time to ask ourselves the most important question? What kind of impact that these electronic devices have on our children or our children's development? Of course not, because a lot of us are not aware of the repercussions, and those who do don't really care. Certainly, without a doubt, the iPhone, iPod, and the computer have some serious negative impact on the children. And it is also true that some of us do use it as a learning method that is fine for a short period of time a day. But it becomes a problem when, as parents, we give priority to these electronic devices in place of other ways of teaching and learning. For sure, it will impact them in a negative way.

When it comes to communicating or engaging a conversation one on one with another person, these kids feel awkward because their communication skills is limited simply because they only know how to e-mail and text and that is deep. I remember when I was growing up in Haiti, I used to play outside and communicate often with my surroundings, but unfortunately, I don't see that anywhere I go because children don't play and communicate anymore. Brothers and sisters, things are changing for the worse, not for the better. That is exactly why social skills are dead. It is because of these electronic devices (no experience, no learning).

There are two ways that children learn, it is through "playing" and observing," said the experts.

Play: by playing with their friends and peers, they gain experience and from experience comes learning.

Observation: children observe what parents do and do the same. They listen to how parents talk and talk the same way. They observe what they do and act the same way. That is what children do because they're copycats. As parents, if we stay on our phone, iPod, and computer almost all day and every day, of course, they are going to do the same because by seeing or watching us doing it, they think that is the right thing to do. Therefore, as adults, our negative attitudes and behaviors do impact our children's development.

Parents, when children spend all day in the house playing video games, watching TV, or on the social media, and they are not outside playing and engaging with their friends when they should, know that something is wrong; and you need to do something about it right away. Because the impact that these electronic devices are having on our children can be significant. Such behavior will distance them from themselves, friends, family members, and parents because they will become so addicted and so used to their screen than people. The more they use their electric devices, the more attached and the more addicted they are getting to them. And that is not healthy and can even have some psychological effects on them according to some experts. Positive and effective communication is extremely important between parents and children. It can make communication more fun and enjoyable when parents and children's relationship is established in a positive way or start on the right track.

No matter how old our children are, positive and effective communication is the best way to building self-esteem without the interruption of technology.

Here are ten components from Vautoir's wall of good intentions that will raise the bar of communication between parents/children that I'm sharing with you.

- The best way to communicate with our children is to put ourselves down to their level when communicating to them. "I am the parent" is no more when it comes to communication. The understanding and respect should come both ways.
- Putting a STOP to all phone calls when we have something important to talk about with our children is the best way to do it because face-to-face communication is the way to go.

- Let the children know that we take interest in everything that is going on in their lives, and we want to be part of it.
- Nothing else matters but our children when they want to communicate or tell us about something that is battering them.
- If our children say or do something to upset us, first thing to do is to keep cool. Do not engage any conversation about the incident or say nothing right away. It is always in our best interest as parents to take a deep breath that will calm us down and talk to them later in private for better results.
- Do not talk to the children in any kind of way in front of others. We will put them in their little shoes (embarrassment). Such negative behavior will take them straight to hostility and resentment (very poor communication).
- If we are dead tired and our children choose the moment to communicate, make an extra effort to be a compassionate listener. I know it is not easy, but all it takes is a little bit of understanding.
- If there is a problem that needs to be solved, make sure that both parents and children find the real solution before you can end the conversation.
- Always praise our children's effort for keeping the door of communication between you guys open by rewarding them with something they like.
- Always show respect to our children in how we talk to them so they can reproduce the same to us as parents.

When Raising Our Children

Children succeed in positive attention because they feel wanted, respected, appreciated, and loved. Many parents think that it is okay to communicate with their children in a negative way than in a positive way. Therefore, negative feedback always come back to haunt them down. And these children become hostile, disrespectful, and have nothing to do with these kind of parents. On the other hand, positive parents who do praise their children help them to grow and strive. These children pay more attention to their parents. They show respect, and they listen and will do their best to please their parents because they care the same way that their parents care about them (reproduction).

"Good boy," "good girl," "good job," "what a way to go," "I am so proud of you," such treatment will encourage them to do the right thing and to be positive at all times. That is parenting at its best.

Here is something good and positive written by an anonymous person that caught my eyes and attention a year ago.

One Final Touch

- If a child lives with criticism, he learns to condemn.
- If a child lives with hostility, he learns to fight.
- If a child lives with ridicule, he learns to be shy.
- If a child lives with fear, he learns to be apprehensive.
- If a child lives with shame, he learns to feel guilty.
- If a child lives with tolerance, he learns to be patient.
- If a child lives with encouragement, he learns to be confident.
- If a child lives with acceptance, he learns to love.
- If a child lives with recognition, he learns it is good to have a goal.
- If a child lives with honesty, he learns what truth is.
- If a child lives with fairness, he learns justice.
- If a child lives with security, he learns to have faith in himself and those about him.
- If a child lives with friendliness, he learns the world is a nice place to love and to be loved.

Personally, I call this the "power of living." Children love to hear how well they are doing, especially from their parents. Positive parents do it in one state of mind which is to boost their children's self-esteem. Such strategy will also shift the children's behaviors toward positive attitudes. Praising your children is also encouraging them to do the right thing and making them proud of themselves. These positive attitudes will only guide them to the right corner of life and help them achieve greatness. Praising them is the best gift ever that parents could give to them. It is also a way to tell your children what kind of attitudes and behaviors that are acceptable and which ones are not. What pleased us as parents and what is not. Trust me, parents, keep praising your children; and if you have not done it yet, now is the time to start so they can grow up with confidence and become responsible adults. It will shift their personality, integrity, and understand what is right and what is wrong—better children, better societies, better families and a better world.

Lying to your Children

Lying to your children is making a liar out of them. Basically, what you are doing as parents, you're teaching them how to lie to you and other people. You are telling them that it is okay to lie, and there is nothing wrong with that. But in the meantime, it is okay to keep a secret from them because not telling them is not lying to them. They are not aware of your past so how can you lie to them when they don't know? Therefore, it's better to keep a secret than lie to your children.

Steve Harvey said,

> Because you have done things in the past that your kids don't need to know about. Matter affect it is best for them not to ever found out because you are trying to raise your kids better than the way you were raised, you want them to have better opportunities than you had. You don't want them to step in the same traps that you stepped into. So now sometimes you have to tell them some but best not to tell them all traps you have stepped into, it's not just best because kids will use it against you, they are manipulative

little devils. "You did it when you were my age, why can't I do it?

Steve Harvey was talking about secrets and lies; therefore, what I have learned from his prospective is that it's good and bad at the same time to lie to your children, meaning it has a good and bad side. For example, Steve says when his son asked him if he used to sneak out the house, he answered, "I never sneak out the house." But in reality, he did. Therefore, he lied to his son. He didn't lie just to lie. He lied because he didn't want his son to end up doing the same thing that he was doing or make the same mistakes that he made. He wants to raise him better and have a better life by teaching his son to do the right thing; such lie is understandable. Compared to Steve Harvey, some parents do tell white lies to their children. For example, if the children ask them if they can go out shopping with them, they might come up with a white lie. "Oh sorry, honey, it's going to rain today so we won't be able to go shopping today because we don't want to get caught in the rain and get sick. You don't want us to get sick now, do you?" Instead of telling the children the real reason why they can't go shopping with them, they might be very busy, or they might have no money (broke). Whatever the case may be, you have to tell the kids the truth; tell them the real inconvenience that you are having and why you are not able to take them shopping, but these parents choose to lie instead. How would you feel when your children see no rain, what then? Now instantly, they will see that they are dealing with liars. And when you messed up like this, your children are going to start losing respect for you. They will call you liars, and they are going to lie to you as well (reproduction).

Experts say, "By lying to your children, it can have long-lasting effects on them. And for the rest of the children lives, they will undermine their ability to trust and somewhat your authority." Some parents lie to their children for no reason at all (white lie). They will say something like, "If you don't stop screaming on top of your longs like this, the police are going to come to get you and place you behind bars. Stop now because they almost here if you don't want to go to jail." There is a possibility that you might or might not get them to stop yelling. What you think is going to happen when the children don't see any police at the door like you have said? Parents, I am telling you today that lying to your children (white lie) is not protecting them.

Matter of fact, it's destroying their self-esteem, their trust, and their respect for you as parents. All you have to do is sit with your children and let them know the reality of life, what is wrong and what is right, what to do, what not to do, what to say, what not to say, what is a lie, what is the truth. By doing so, you are preparing real soldiers for the modern world. Parenting at its best.

The Effects of Negative Talk

- Negative talk is very harmful to the listener or the addresser. It brings about anger, hate, pain, and suffering.
- If the kind of conversation you are having is mean and offensive, there will be negative consequences. Therefore, such anomaly can lead to big arguments, fights, word exchange, etc.
- Negative communication can turn into violence. And when violence is present, anything bad can happen. So let us, as human beings, make an effort to be more positive than negative in what we say and do to others. By doing so, we will bring blessing upon us and others.
- Negative thinking can have a deadly impact on communication. With a positive thinking that can only offer us positive attitude on a silver platter is telling us that negative communication can be changed into positive for the sake of the pain and suffering of others. Negative attitude does not achieve greatness and success. Only a positive mind-set does.
- You are what you think you are. You can achieve whatever you want to achieve in life in a positive mind-set. This pandemic called negativity can crush your life and your future into little pieces where no one is going to recognize

you anymore. You will end up lost, confused, beaten up, smashed, and lonely; and nobody will be able to help you. You are done.

The Fatherless Syndrome

Growing up without a father for these young men and women around the world, especially in the United States of America, is worse than the COVID-19. I found out 80 percent of teen pregnancy in America came from fatherless homes. These children have no understanding whatsoever what a father is about because they never have one in their lives; therefore, it left them with a scar called father wound that impacted the lives of those innocent kids and their future relationships with others in so many ways. It is a world of pandemic that is destroying the children around the globe because they are hopeless, hopeless because the love of their birth father is nowhere to be found and causing them to think very low of themselves (low self-esteem), which make them think that they are unwanted. Such negative feeling creates a deep emotional pain and suffering inside of each and every one of them.

These children are neglected and taken for granted by so-called fathers. When I analyzed and envision what these fatherless children are going and been through across the United States of America and around the world, my heart dropped, and that is why I came up with Vautoir's antidote so they can receive the healing they need and deserve. They will heal from pain and suffering, negative feelings such as low self-esteem, hate, thinking that they are unwanted, stupid, unimportant, unloved, incompetent, unworthy, etc. my antidote will help them to understand and see things differently so they can become new people with new thinking, new ideas and new lives.

In my research, I found out that they are 24 million children without a father in America alone. Now that is a huge number of children who do not have a clue what their fathers look like or who just see their fathers occasionally, and that is deep. It is deep because it is more trouble for the world, every state, every city, every country, and every nation on earth if something is not done about this worldwide pandemic. I grew up without a father myself. I have no idea how he looks like, no picture, no souvenir, but his name. And that is hard to swallow. That is exactly why I am in my kids' life. And I am not going anywhere, and we're so stuck together. Also, I will, in the future, father other children so I can heal their wounds while giving them another direction or sense of life because it is an affirmation that every single human being must have in their life (father figure). The fatherless wound is something that no child should have experienced. It is very painful. This pandemic exists in the ghettos, suburban. It has no gender, no preferences, and no color and have no boundaries. And that is why, as concern citizens, we have to do everything in our power to break this evil cycle of fatherless all over the world. The happiness and the health of the children are at stake.

When I was growing up, I made a promise to myself to be always there for my children and make sure that they do not go through what I went through. I always work independently so I can keep my eyes on them. Did it come with consequences? Of course, it did because I did not make the kind of money that I wanted, but I have my kids because I saved them from lots of bad things that could happen to them or involved in. That is way much greater than money. It is better to make less money and raise your children the right way and be there for them when they need you the most. Making a lot of money and losing my children was not an option for me. Is it really worth it to make a lot of money and lose your children? Is it really worth it to make a lot of money and have no one to share it with? Children growing up without a father in the house are more likely to grow up in poverty and drop out of school. It is inevitable. Unfortunately, over 3,200-plus young men and women dropout every day in the United States of America.

- The US ranks 22 of 27 develop countries for percentage of youth who graduated from high school.
- 71 percent of youth that drop out came from fatherless homes.

- 75 percent of all crimes are committed by high school drop outs.
- 85 percent of all youth in prison came from fatherless homes.

Almost a quarter of American children under eighteen years of age live with a single parent, study has proven; in comparison, 3 percent of children in China, 4 percent of children in Nigeria, and 5 percent of children in India live in single-parent households. In neighboring Canada, the share is 15 percent.

The fact of the matter is this pandemic called "fatherless syndrome" is paralyzing our children and societies. A huge number of Latino, white, and brown-skinned children are growing up in fatherless homes in America. By looking at the facts, we can say that our culture is shifting away from marriages, relationships, responsibility, love, compassion, humility, respect, family values; and the innocent children are paying the price. All the good moral values that we had in the past is melting away right before our eyes. We feel helpless, and the devil is smiling.

Seriously, the United States of America has to come with a solution ASAP against this syndrome. If my formula is chosen, that would be awesome. If it is rejected, America has to come right away with their own to save marriages, relationships, and the American children. This fatherless syndrome cannot continue putting America and other countries around the world on their knees like this. Something has to be done now. I strongly believe that the antidote that I propose is the best to save America and the world from this terrible disease that is turning the life of the children into a nightmare, and that is dividing families (divorce). Let us, as a people and concerned citizens, look for real solutions together so we can destroy this pandemic before it is too late. If we decide to take such initiative, it will bring peace of mind upon the children, families, marriages, and relationships. It is extremely important as concerned American citizens that we take care of our country, children, and our nation because nobody else will come and do it for us. Plus, we are the first country and nation in the world. That is why we should be a living example for the others. Therefore, it is urgent and important that we do our best to eradicate this syndrome in our society for good.

Fathers who engage in the lives of their children will be blessed by the Almighty God. And this is the best gift ever that a father could give to his children. It eliminates all doubts, negative feelings, and emotions that the children may have and bring on positive vibes. The real anomaly here is that too many young men and young women don't know and don't want to know, don't hear and don't want to hear the Word of God. And as a result, we are all paying the consequences. Most of them didn't raise with the Word of God because they didn't have anybody to teach them or simply because no one took the time to teach them. As good parents, we have the obligation to rethink and react on behalf of our children because their happiness, health, and their future are at stake.

May the understanding, the compassion, and the love that we must have be with us all as parents and concerned citizens in America and around the world so we can save the children (one love).

A Good Father

A good father doesn't mean paying child support for your children, or meeting your financial obligations doesn't make you a good father. It doesn't have anything at all to do with it. When it comes to money, it's not important at this point. It's simply what they want and need that matters, and what they really after is your time. They want their dads to spend quality time with them so you can get to know each other and communicate more. Unfortunately, for some mothers, if the father becomes unemployed and misses a payment of his child support, the access to see his children is automatically denied by the mother which went back and hunt the children. These kids became a boutique for such mothers (no money, can't see the children), and when it comes to money, these moms don't care (money first, children second). The worse scenario is that they don't even spend the child support money on the children. They spend it on themselves and their boyfriends. For some, financial support is not that important. They just need responsible fathers that will spend quality time and be there for their children when they need them the most. A good father should be there for their children physically, emotionally, and spiritually so they can guide them to the right path.

Here are seven attributes from Vautoir's wall of good intensions that all good dads should possess that I'm sharing with you.

- Affection
  A good father always cherish his children and also hugging and kissing them and telling them how much they love them and how smart they are from time to time.
- Patience
  A good father is always patient with his children and listen to them with open ears (deep listening).
- Respect
  A good father always shows respect to his children no matter what so they can reproduce.
- Provider
  A good father always provides for his children. That's a responsible father.
- Protection
  A good father always protects his children, even die for them.
- Live
  A good father always lives by example a role model.
- Commitment
  A good father always commits to his children 24-7, be there for them whenever.

Every child wants to have a hero in their life, and the first person that they look up to is their loving father. Therefore, when problems find its place in the family and split such family, Father went his way and Mom her way, know that the children's life also split because there're certain things that start to happen to the kids, such as a lack of confidence, finding identity, low-self-esteem; and believe me, that's a huge change. A good father is someone who takes time to raise his children the right way and makes the difference in their lives. He protects, disciplines, and guides them through life so in the future, they can become well-adjusted adults. It is also a way to STOP them from becoming a disgrace to the family and their surroundings. A good father always loves and cares for his children and makes sure that they don't turn out to be gang members, thieves, rapists, liars, and killers. When a father steps up and takes good care of his family, especially his children, he leaves no room for thugs, low lives, and losers to take part in his family because he wants them to strive and become good citizens. He loves his children with unconditional love, forever love. Each and every father in this world has a crucial role to play in the physical, emotional, social, and spiritual development of their sons and daughters. They're supposed to be responsible, supportive, and affectionate to their loved ones.

Proverbs 3:11–12, the Lord says, "My son, do not despise the Lord's discipline, and do not resent his rebuke, because the Lord disciplines those he loves, as a father the son he delights in." Most men in the world, like myself, would like to be good fathers, but unfortunately many of us don't know our fathers or didn't raise by one. Therefore, chances are we never really have a father that sat down with us and taught us how to be or become great dads. Does it mean that we can't become one? Of course not, we can become the best dad ever without being taught how to become one because "where there's a will, there is a way." And it doesn't necessarily mean that we want to be just like our fathers, do what they did, talk as they talked, solve problems as they did, and have the same habit that they had because we are our own persons, plus we are different and unique. We just wanted for them to be there for us so they could teach us what's good and what's not, what to do and what not to do like normal children have, to install in us some moral values and teach us how to be positive and do the right thing. Such teaching would give us some light how to raise our children our own way. Such strategy would also improve our relationship with our children and spouses for better families. And with such a positive attitude and behavior, it would raise the bar of our self-awareness. It would give us the power and enough knowledge to define the real meaning of fatherhood each and every day in our lives. That's exactly how we would set great example and became real role models for our own children so they can pass it on from generation to generation that would give us better fathers, better mothers, better children, better citizens, better nations, better countries, and a better world for sure where people would be safer and happier, and peace would be in all families. That's exactly the kind of movement we need in America and around the world, better fathering. I am not a good father at all. I'm just trying, and that's why I have to learn every day how to become one and a better one.

So here are forty-one ways to be a better father from Vautoir's wall of good intentions on fatherhood that I am sharing with you.

- Always give your kids a hug and a kiss from time to time. When you go home, tell them how much you missed them and love them.
- Be there for them when they need you. It's the least you can do.
- Make sure that you praise them every single day.
- Try your best to create your own little world with your family (family time). Close your business. Call out to be with your family; family matters.
- Be a living example for your children by trying your best to improve your relationships or marriages.
- Make sure that you trash all negativity when you are with your children. It's really contagious; therefore, focus on positivity only.
- Wash the dishes, broom, and mop the house when you can because they are watching you. They got their eyes on you. Be a role model.
- Always find time to play, laugh, and enjoy your children. They deserve it.
- Throw away your electronic devices when it comes to your children.
- Make sure that your children read more than sitting in front of a TV, computer, or playing video games day and night.

- Take your blame for your mistake. Know when you are wrong, and learn to apologize. Don't say they are just kids, big mistake.
- Teach them the importance of forgiveness and what God said about it.
- Learn to leave your trash at work. Please don't take it home with you and dump it on your children and wives. They are no dumpster.
- Make sure you are aware of what your children want and don't want, what they like and don't like. It is extremely important that you know your own children.
- Teach them the importance of respect, compassion, and understanding others. It will be their ticket to a successful future.
- Always place yourself in a position to help others, especially the unfortunate ones, so they can do the same.
- Make sure that you teach them about saving, not spending.
- Always ask them for advice. They will feel important and valued.
- Never give up, never quit, and they will do the exact same thing.
- It's okay to make mistake, everyone does; it's in our DNA. But don't keep reaping the same mistake over and over again so it doesn't become a problem.
- As parents, make sure that you stand in the same corner. When dad says no, it is no; and when mom says yes, it is yes. The decisions can't be different; otherwise, it will bring disrespect and hostility in the family.
- Show respect toward one another in the house so the kids can grow up and be respectful adults.
- Act in a way so that they see you care and appreciate them.
- Take time to teach and communicate positively with your children.
- Keep a smile on your face no matter what the circumstances may be.

- Show your children that they are everything to you, and you cannot live without them.
- Make every day your last day. Make it count. Live it to the fullest.
- It is okay to cry when your feelings are hurt or when you find yourselves in a deep sadness.
- Take a walk with your children and learn from them while you're teaching them.
- Tell them that it's vital to tell the truth at all times because the hole of lies is not deep at all.
- Teach them the importance of trust.
- Let them know that they can accomplish whatever they put their mind to.
- Never stop joking and fooling around with your children.
- Never choose for your children. Let them make their own choice. You can only advise them, not dictate.
- Make sure that you don't drop your heavy loads on their shoulders. Your problems are yours and make sure they stay yours.
- Do not accuse without any tangible proof. Try to use some common sense when dealing with your children.
- Always keep your promises. Live by your words. Your words are your bonds, your passport, and your ID, can't live without them.
- Give your wives a break from time to time by taking over their duties.
- Be generous with your money. Give, share, and donate to the less fortunate so your children can follow your footsteps. They will learn not everybody is fortunate, and they will love others.
- Let them know that they have to study and work real hard for everything that they want and need. Nothing is for free in this world.
- Let them know that their personality, dignity, and integrity are not for sale. And that's the only thing that they will take with them to the grave, not money nor power.

It is way much better to commit to your wives and children, brothers, than yourselves. By doing so, you are teaching them not to be selfish and that families come first. Good fathers usually see their children instead of themselves and other females, and they refuse to be skirt runners. They also know that they have their families to take care and try their best to save their souls. Good dads always want to keep their families together and try their best to make it happen.

They always put God first before themselves, children and wives (family that pray together stay together). A good father is also a man that values himself, his children, and wife or the mother of his children, a man who doesn't choose pleasure and other women over his family, a responsible man, a man with great character, personality, and dignity that allows him to respect his children and wife and make a positive difference in their lives.

A father supports, loves, and guides his children so they can be very successful and achieve greatness. Unfortunately, good fathers are very hard to find nowadays. Too many men are diving in the deep pool of fatherless and don't come back to surface and drown because they feel as though they can't or don't know how to accomplish their duties as fathers. It's not an easy task but an effort has to be made in order to STOP this fatherless pandemic around the world. Be loyal and stay loyal because loyalty is the bridge that keeps families together where either partners or spouses in a relationship or marriage don't have to worry about cheating. And each partner or spouse is here today, will be there tomorrow and forever for one another. That's what I call real commitment, and that's what a good father does—he commits to his wife and children; he sticks to his words, choices, and promises. Loyal fathers don't value work, friendship, pleasure, and other women more than their families.

There are many different things that define a good father along with that for the success and development of the children and marriages. Therefore, the attitudes and behaviors of the father are an essential piece in the puzzle. It's unfortunate that today's societies do not value the importance of a father in the life of his children and how the absence of the fathers is torturing the children around the world. A good father loves and protects his children and wife.

It's a lighting path with candles to a long-lasting relationship and marriage. A good dad knows the importance of disciplining his children. He knows also discipline them is not only for today but for tomorrow also so they can grow up and become responsible adults. A good father also know that he has to lead by example by being a real leader in the house—can't lead nothing else if you can't lead your own home. He teaches his children how to be polite and respectful, and he can't do otherwise (practice what you preach). He can't tell his children not to drink and smoke and practice them himself. Such attitude would teach them how to be dishonest and would automatically see him as a liar and a hypocrite. A good father doesn't want that. He wants to be a role model for his children and wife. Also he always put his family first, and such antidote will cure any household from any "fatherless syndrome."

Ex-president barrack Obama said, "We need fathers to realize that responsibility doesn't end at conception. We need them to realize that what makes you a man is not the ability to have a child—it's the courage to raise one."

Irresponsible fathers are the ones who don't take time or are never present in their children's lives. They refuse to understand the importance of fatherhood by continuously neglecting their own flesh and blood. They are clueless of what the duty of a father is which is to love, protect, support, and guide their children through their journey. They are very irresponsible individuals who have no sense of what being a father really is. For those who have a chance to spend time with their children, set very bad example for them. They sell drugs in front of them. They have multiple girlfriends that are coming and going out the house. They tell the kids not to talk behind people's back, and they are the first one doing it. They will also tell them to respect everybody. They will be the first one to disrespect their children and others.

How can you be a living example or a role model for your children by doing the exact same thing you've told them not to do right before their eyes? They don't respect their words and their promises. They have no will to do what's right. They beat up their kids whenever they feel like it, no reason whatsoever. They only know how to use violence to impose rules and regulations without any understanding by using force or violence that they are teaching their kids; aggression is the best way to deal with conflict. They don't only abuse them physically but emotionally, mentally, and sexually. Some take pleasure in ripping their own children, even have babies by them, very evil fathers, just like Trazen Georges with his stepdaughter Sherwin who had an abortion for him according to a source that I give credit to. Some refuse to create time and go places with their children because they think it's not important or telling themselves that they don't have time. They don't understand that by having such negative attitude and behavior toward their children will make them believe that they are not important, they have no value, and they are unwanted. They choose to please others but their families.

These bad fathers are very toxic and dysfunctional, and unfortunately, many children grow up with such fathers and follow their footsteps. When they become adults, some of them try will hard to be different from their fathers, but "the blood calls the blood." There's a fair chance that the same negative behavior can still manifest in their lives. Those children grow up and become adults, living a stressful and unhappy life because their fathers used to call them all kind of names, abused them and blame them for everything. They always take home with them their problems such as having a bad day, being broke, unemployed, hardship, etc. It's possible that all these negative feelings or sense of guilt can follow them through adulthood. They always think that it's their fault and blaming themselves for everything, even take it on their wives and children when they don't have anything to do with it, very unfair.

Love and affection isn't a constant factor in their lives; therefore, they find themselves searching for it at every corner of their lives except in their families. They determine to please everybody outside their families while saying yes to everything they are told or asked, always ending up buying things that they can't afford just to please a friend or girlfriend. They become overly generous with their time and money to people that they want to impress. Believe me, such pleasing behavior doesn't make them happy at all. It just make them look stupid, miserable, feeling guilty, and burned down. In their state of mind, pleasing other people will make them think highly of them so they can feel good about themselves. Unfortunately, it's not easy to get what you desire in life. Plus, whatever you do, you will never be able to please everyone in the world; and if you think you can, you're just a fool. First and foremost, try to please God first and yourself, then your family. Trust and believe, that's exactly where the happiness you're looking for is hiding. This toxic cycle needs to be broken because your own children don't have to pay the price of your negative childhood. You are your own person. You are not your parents, and you will never be.

Here are ten components of Vautoir's wall of good intentions on how to treat your children that I'm sharing with you.

- See your children in a way that you parents didn't see you—positive way.
- Treat them in a way that you parents never treat you.
- Make your children proud of you.
- Communicate with them in a way that your parents never did to you.
- Do for them what your parents never did for you.
- Love them in a way that your parents never love you.
- Give them what your parents never gave you.
- Take them places that your parents never took you.
- Always tell them how smart they are.
- Let them know that they can accomplish anything in life as long as they put their mind to it.

It's unfortunate to see that many fathers these days choose doing to their kids what their fathers used to do to them (like father like son). They scream, beat, rip, punch, and kick their children; they have no affection whatsoever. They don't make any effort to be different from their abusive fathers, at the same time to make a conscious decision to turn these negative behaviors into positive ones. For example, instead of yelling at your children that say or do something that they have no business of saying or doing, you communicate with them rather than screaming your lungs at them or hurt them. That's being an irresponsible father. They don't understand if they communicate with their children. Their negative thoughts, attitudes, and behaviors would automatically turn into positive ones. Communication takes you to a constructive path, not a destructive one. Be aware.

I know that your wounds from your toxic father's behaviors will take time to heal, but at the same time, it's vital that you put a STOP to repeating unhealthy and unhappy patterns of your past or your nightmares, causing your children to suffer. You have to remain firm as the head of your household in your efforts to better yourselves and your families and turn your children into the persons you wish you were when you were kids yourselves. Know that your past experience will hunt you down and will affect you, your surroundings, and your families. The best thing to do in order to avoid such nightmare is to open your doors to change and positivity.

As they say, "Negative children come from negative parents." And there are multiple ways to be a negative parent. Parents are a child's best teacher ever; a child's behavior, goal, respect, passion, and attitude come from nobody else but their parents. Parents can raise smart children. They can also raise losers depending how they've been raised and what they've been taught. The method that parents used to raise their children and what they learn in that process or the experience that they're facing will live a remarkable impression on them for a lifetime. That's why it's imperative, more than an obligation, to raise the children the right way. Good parenting is a must. When a child becomes a disgrace to the family and the society that he/she is part of, or simply has bad manners, the blame always locates the parents or parent because they are responsible to teach them what's right and what's wrong so they can become good citizens. Society always looks at child attitude and behavior so they can know or say to themselves if such child has good or bad parents. It's clear like a crystal or coconut water that bad parenting has bad consequences on the children around the world, and such pandemic comes mostly from bad fathers who refuse to take responsibility of their own actions.

Here are fifteen signs from Vautoir's wall of good intentions that will help you define a bad from a good father that I'm sharing with you.

- When a father doesn't live by his words
- When a father loves one of his children more than the others
- When a father abuses sexually, physically, and verbally his children
- When a father refuses to take care or turn his back on his children
- When a father doesn't value his children
- When a father doesn't trust his children
- When a father is using fear and violence in the family
- When a father is lacking of communication
- When a father is not trustworthy
- When a father lies to his family
- When a father only cares about his work and money
- When a father doesn't hug and kiss his children
- When a father never says to his children that he loves them
- When a father never says to his children how much he misses them
- When a father never creates time for his children

As a father myself, I'm begging all fathers around the world, please STOP neglecting your children for God's sake. It can affect them in a very negative way. It's also a form of abuse that can be worse than physical abuse from what I see and know. When you neglect your children, you ignore their needs and wants and turn your back on them in dangerous situations where they feel worthless. Neglecting your children will force them to live a very unstable, unhealthy, and unhappy life that will leave them with a wound that will take a lifetime to heal and will be accompanied by psychological scars. Neglecting your children is teaching them that loneliness is the way of life. There are a lot of negative things that are related to neglect such as negative attitudes, behaviors, isolation, low self-esteem, stealing, anger, hate, depression, stress, crime, become gang members, and poor learning, etc. When children don't get the attention that they deserve, they will do anything that they can think of to get it, including murder. And it might be very difficult for them to maintain healthy and happy relationships or marriages. Every child on earth deserves to be loved and cherished by their parents. That's why, as a man, I'm reaching to the baby makers out there to STOP being baby makers and step into the world of fatherhood so they can become real fathers for the well-being of the children around the world. Prioritize your children by taking time to talk to them, and to get to know them is the best you can do for them. The bond between you and your children is there. You don't have to look far. Make sure that you treat them with respect so they can feel loved, appreciated, and protected (children count).

Let me justify for a moment what I mean by "baby makers," if I may. I will make the difference between baby makers and real fathers.

- Baby makers are individuals who think that they are men but only have the ability to make babies. But not quite men yet because they don't know the real meaning of commitment and are very irresponsible. They also use a very toxic language when addressing to their children and baby mamas or their wives. They have no understanding of what love really is.
- Real fathers are good and responsible men that make sure that the heath and the happiness of their children are not at stake, men that stick to their promises and words and that provide for their families and assure that they are loved and safe, men that talk to their wives and children with respect, love, and compassion, men that always show kindness and humility no matter what the circumstances may be.

To me, that's what a real father is. I call the irresponsible ones "baby makers" because they are spreading their diseases all across America and around the world. They lay their eggs in almost every family called fatherless syndrome. This pandemic is destroying children all over the world and turns their lives into a nightmare. Some children become drug addicts, drug dealers, alcoholic, suicidal, etc. It's up to the concerned citizens of this world to come together and do something about this horrifying situation for better families, and the time is now.

Successful Families

Successful families are husbands and wives that understand what they have going on. They see it as a commitment and a permanent bond that creates a sense of security between the couple. And each one of them strongly believes that no matter what such union brings, it will be honored by both spouses. Far better, they understand the real meaning of relationship and marriage. They understand that it's a sense of commitment that is based on mutual love and respect. Therefore, being committed to their engagement allows themselves to be successful. By being quick to forgive and apologize also allows the couple to live happily ever after.

In 1 Corinthians 7:11, God said, "A husband should not leave his wife." No one can avoid problems or trouble. No matter what, they will always be there. Matter a fact, trouble is the last name of life. When problems knock at their doors because of their commitment and their bond, they look for solutions as a real team. But for those who are not committed to each other are more likely to conclude "this isn't going to work" and take the easiest route (divorce). Teamwork in a marriage says a lot. Both husband and wife know working together head-to-head and hands in hands will give better results that will take them on the path of successful families. Every good husband and wife know that marriage is not a one-way street, and it's a long journey so they have to work hard in a certain unity in order to flip it into a wonderful and awesome journey. Couples who are bonded and committed to one another don't worry about who's right and who's wrong. Their only concern is to find a way to bring peace and prosperity in their marriage. Also they don't see money as mine but as ours so they can keep a healthy and happy marriage.

They always communicate to each other in a respectful way because they care and love each other, even during a disagreement. To tell you the truth, positive couples don't argue. They communicate with each other about differences and conflicts (mutual respect). They listen to each other's perspective in a respectful way and try their best to find solutions that work for each spouse.

That's what love and marriage is all about. It's never about my personal interest, and it should never be. It's about our interest because we are one. They respect each other; therefore, they value one another and don't want to do anything that would sabotage their marriage and would put them into pain and suffering. With a lack of respect, communication among husbands and wives can be filled of criticism and sarcasm that can lead them to divorce. That's exactly why those who are committed to each other choose to respect one another for the well-being of their marriage. God said, "Clothe yourselves with the tender affections of compassion, kindness, humility, mildness and patience" (Colossians 3:12).

Commitment is a responsibility and a choice. Remember to fulfill it with honor. They're quick to forgive because they know with forgiveness the torch that they hold on the path of each other will never die. To forgive means to let go of an offense or mistake, also any negative feelings or resentment it may have caused. Forgiveness doesn't mean neither to pretend like nothing never happened. They forgive each other because they know the repercussion of it (forgive to be forgiven). They forgive one another for a long-lasting marriage or relationship. They understand that when you're madly in love with someone, you don't look through every little mistake that person makes. Instead, they look at the bright side, not the dark side. They always value the effort of one another to make things better while looking also to see the kind of person that he/she wants to be. They don't hold resentment by knowing that they can hurt themselves physically and emotionally, and they can poison their marriages or relationships.

They also learn not to blame each other; "It's your fault. No, it's your fault." They really don't have time for negative vibes. In their state of mind, they know it's easy to forgive when they place themselves in the same basket (meaning for them, it's way much easier to forgive when both spouses are at fault instead of pointing fingers. If that's not true humility, I don't know what is). What I have learned through my seventeen going on eighteen years of marriage, I have learned that forgiveness can put out the flame or the heat in all marriages or relationships where conflicts, arguments, hostilities, resentments, emotions, and disrespect will become powerless. Successful families are also aware that communication takes place in the families when feelings and thoughts are shared between spouses. Therefore, they value communication a whole lot because they know it can be very challenging. The couples focus on communication as an essential tool in their marriages or relationships. They value each other's feelings. They know when to listen, when to talk, what to say, and what not to say because they don't want to hurt each other's feelings. These families know the importance of communication, and without it, their marriages or relationships will go down the drain.

The First Epistle to the Corinthians 10:24 stated, "Let each one keep seeking, not his own advantage, but that of the other person." I want you to know and understand that communication is the bridge that will keep both spouses connected to a better future. These kinds of families are very strict with their children and know how to discipline them (hate me today and love me tomorrow). When it comes to discipline, it means to guide and to teach. It will correct negative behaviors and impose moral training that will help the children how to make good choices for a better tomorrow. Children need rules and regulations to abide by; but unfortunately, in many households in the United States of America, parents are scared to discipline their children so they don't get in trouble with the law, the law that takes the parenting rights and pass it on to the children. Children need boundaries to help them grow into responsible adults. Without discipline, children are lost and grow up becoming gangsters, drug dealers, drug users, alcoholics, criminals, rapists, thieves, and professional liars.

CHAPTER 4

Domestic Violence

As we all know, domestic violence is a serious threat to some women and men around the world. No one told them that the women or men they have a relationship with or married to would become their nightmares. Such negative behavior is used by one partner or spouse to intimidate, to be in control, or to maintain power over the other person in an intimate relationship or marriage. Anyone can be a victim because domestic violence doesn't care if you are a beggar or a millionaire, tall or short, beautiful or ugly, brown-skinned or white, age, religion, sexual orientation, or gender. It doesn't discriminate. Anybody can be an offender or a victim of domestic violence. It can happen to educated or uneducated people, and it doesn't matter where you come from and who you are.

There're six types of domestic violence that the abusive partner or offender can use to STOP the other partner or spouse from doing what she wishes or to force her to do what she doesn't want to do.

- Threats and intimidation
    They use such tactic to place fear in their partner or spouse so they can do what they're told. And that's where the offender gets his power and control.

- Physical harm

    That's when the abusive partner or spouse punches and kicks you, and such violence can result in death or bruises.
- Sexual violence

    It's unlawful for anyone to engage or to force someone to have sex. But the abusive partner or spouse act in that way from time to time which is a negative behavior.
- Emotional abuse

    An emotional abuse is one that is not physical. It's a stimulus package carried by the abuser—manipulation, intimidation, fear, threats, and humiliation. Such package is carried out by the offender to diminish or minimize the other partner's sense of identity, personality, integrity, dignity, and self-worth which often result in depression, stress, and anxiety!
- Economic abuse

    Economic abuse is when the abusive partner or spouse doesn't allow you to have money in your possession. He will not give you any money, or he might give you just little something out of your pay check that you work hard for!
- Verbal abuse

    Verbal abuse is when the offender repeatedly uses tone and other tactics to scare you such as yelling, blame, criticism, accusations, etc., so he or she can be in control or control a particular person.

Domestic violence takes place when there's a close relationship between the offender and the victim. Anyone can be an abuser or a victim, and it can have a devastating effect on the victim's health. It's extremely important that we understand clearly what domestic violence is all about. Sometimes, the abusers may not even realize that they're applying domestic violence on their partners or spouses. On the other side of the coin, when flipped, victims may not want to take action against their offenders if they're not aware that the nightmare they're living day and night is indeed domestic violence. The more people know about domestic violence, the better chance they have to help the victims or themselves. Also people need to know that domestic violence can take many different forms. A long time ago, domestic violence was referred to as wife abuse. However, such meaning was erased from the board when the definition of domestic violence was changed to consider that wives were not the only ones who can live such nightmare. There're other category of people who are also victims of domestic violence such as spouses, children, intimate partners, family members, dating an abuser, etc.

Be aware that many different forms of abuse or negative behavior give, as result, domestic violence. It's a crime that brings sadness and damage to everyone who is a victim. Please seek for help by calling the National Domestic Violence hotline (1800-799-7233).

Characteristics of Domestic Violence

Here are some signs that will lighten you up when it comes to domestic violence.

- When the abuser threatens to take your children away and tells you that you will never see them again or threatens to kill you or your children.
- When he grabs and pushes you around.
- When he slaps and kicks you.
- When he throws object at you that can cut or hurt you.
- When he starts destroying your belongings or valuables.
- When he uses tactics to intimidate you.
- When he wants you to be lonely, have no friends.
- When he wants to have you under his thumb, meaning control your life.
- When he puts your life in danger by pulling a gun or a knife on you.

Everybody in the world deserve to feel valued, loved, respected, and safe. Therefore, when you're in a relationship or marriage, your first step to be free is to be aware that your relationship or marriage is abusive. Also your inner thoughts and feelings can tell you if you're in an abusive relationship or marriage, know that abusive behavior is a choice.

Here are three elements of abusive behaviors from Vautoir's wall of good intentions that I'm sharing with you.

- Dominance

    First and foremost, the abuser wants to be in charge of the marriage or relationship. They enjoy telling you what to do and when to do it, where to go and where not to go. Your offender may sometimes treat you like a maid or like a child, even like a slave because he takes pleasure in doing it.

- Isolation

    In order for you to depend on them more and more every day, the offender will close and lock the gate so he can cut you off of all contacts (no friends, no visit from family members, can't go to school or work). For you to do something or go somewhere, you have to ask permission first. With the abuser, there's no out-of-jail free card unless you choose to run away for good.

- Humiliation

    An offender will do anything in his power to make you feel worthless, to minimize you, and to lower your self-esteem so he can prove to you that you are nobody. He just wants to place you in a state of mind so you can doubt yourself and believe that you're nothing. He knows that if he makes you believe all these negative thoughts and feelings, you're less likely to leave him. All these tactics and name-calling are designed to make you feel powerless.

Please, brothers and sisters, if you know or suspect someone you know or don't know is being abused, it can be a friend, a sibling, a coworker, or even a total stranger, say something, do something, or call the police or the National Domestic Violence hotline that I provided. Don't say "it's not my concern or my business" because it is. You can save a life by participating directly or indirectly. We have to learn to care and protect each other as God's creations, and it will send a clear message to the victim that you're different and you care about others. Tell the victim that if she needs further assistance or need someone to talk to, that you're here for her. One thing that I really want you to know, brothers and sisters, is that the abusers are very good at what they do, very slake people. They're very good in manipulating and controlling their victims. Therefore, the victims need every little help that they can get to pull them out of such nightmare.

The victims usually feel stressed, depressed, confused, and scared after they been emotionally, mentally, and physically abused. For the women out there worldwide who are in abusive relationships, believe me, I know what you're going through, and it's not easy for you. But you deserve to live free from violence and fear. You certainly deserve better treatment because the kind of treatment or abuse that you're receiving from your men is unacceptable. Even animals shouldn't have such treatment. Some people always say to themselves or to others, "Why is she still with him? Why doesn't she leave?" Let me tell you something, it's not that simple. Putting an end to something that you spend all of your energy and time and spend years to build is not easy at all, especially when the abusers closed each and every door and locked the victims in so they can't see their friends and family members. These tactics are used to scare and intimidate the victims. Also, it's a way to maintain control. Some offenders make it very hard for the victims to leave them because they place fear in them. The victims have been told, "If you make an attempt to leave, I will kill you and the children," or something like, "If you leave me, I will find you and make you pay," things of this nature.

But I have to say also that some women choose to stay with their abusers because of what they represent in the society or by simply trying to protect their names and reputation. Let me give you a very sad example: There was a very talented lady, a Haitian Christian singer named Sister Rose. She was married to Trezan Georges whom everybody called Pastor Georges. Sister Rose Georges was traumatized, humiliated by devil Georges secretly or in private to a point where she fell and have a stroke by holding everything inside and kept the outsiders out of her business. Therefore, beside the stroke, everybody thought that everything was going well for her and her family when in reality, she was living a nightmare with her so-called husband. He controlled and forced her to have concert after her first stroke so that he can take all of the money as he always does, so Rose was psychologically beaten down and financially controlled. When Sister Rose couldn't take it anymore and asked him to go and get a job, his response was, "Why would I go and punch in when I have a talented woman like yourself? All you have to do is keep singing and make me some money." He is a very lazy individual who refused to work, relied on her wife to put money in his pockets. When it's therapy time, he will take her without washing or bathing her. When she requested that he does, he said he doesn't have time for that. And most of the time, Trezan Georges took her to therapy with no underwear. Georges even lied to the four children by telling them that their mother had another man; therefore, he told them that "you no longer have a mother" so the children never spoke to their mother since then. He turned the children against their own mother who is innocent of such accusation. He did it just to hurt the mother.

Georges put his wife out of the house in Orlando, and she didn't have anywhere to go. But someone in Canada that she thought was a friend put a big chain and a lock on her refrigerator so Sister Rose didn't touch her food and water. These are the kinds of people who are making it so ugly for real Christians because they call themselves Christians too, and not only that they believe they are when they are nothing else but the devil's agents. So it didn't work out for her. She went back home, and the first thing that the money monster Georges or (cookie monster) told her was, "Did you bring some money with you? If not, go back where you came from right now." Sister Rose continued to sing, traveled many countries while she was disabled, and made money for money monster Georges. The therapist told Sister Rose to have more sex because it's a good therapy for her, and when she told money monster Georges about it, he demanded that she paid, if not, no service. The worse thing of all is that one day, Sister Rose went out; and on her way back home, to her astonishment, she saw Georges and Sherwin were having sex. Sherwin is Sister Rose's daughter, who is Georges' stepdaughter, so she was having an affair with her stepfather. Sister Rose down the road had a second stroke and ran to the hospital with her; but unfortunately, she didn't make it and died on August 7, 2020. Georges took the children and went to a Haitian radio station in Orlando while he stayed hiding in a room of this radio station, and the children were begging for donation so they can bury their mother. They got all together $30,000 so they can bury their mother. At the mother's funeral, the son declared that it was her mother's fault and his dad has nothing to do with what his mom went through. Even after Sister Rose's death, her children still couldn't say anything positive about her because they were brainwashed by the father.

The good thing about all that is that Sister Rose, before she had the second stroke, told a brother of her church everything including the kind of life she was living and how Georges mistreated her and abused her mentally and emotionally, and the brother recorded everything and put it out there. See, what Georges and his lover Sherwin don't understand is that what goes around comes around. Everything that you do on this planet earth has consequences, good or bad. "Both of you are going to pay for what you did to Sister Rose, especially you, Sherwin, after not talking to your mom for two years because you wanted your stepfather, who is your man, all by yourself. So you did find a way to kill her so you can have your man all by yourself. You even have an abortion for Georges, and that's exactly why your breasts are looking at your knees and saying hi. Georges crash them to a point where they are considered as total lost. It will be very difficult for you to find a real man after what you did. Yes, you will find some men that will come and taste the food and walk, and that's about it because no men will take you seriously after you did what you did. You will be a miserable and lonely person all your life; watch and see. Your children are going to live a very difficult life for what you did to your mother. It will follow you through your career, education, etc. All of you have a debt to pay before you die, and you will pay it no matter what, and shame on you for life."

In life, some people are working very hard to go to paradise and others to go to hell. We choose our own path and our own faith; we can be God's children or the devil's agent. It's up to us, and that's why God gave us the right to choose freely. Be aware, the agents of the devil are everywhere (in the churches, in the schools, hospitals, government, families, and workplaces, etc.). We need to learn how to treat others and how to prevent pain and suffering that we're causing to others and how important it is to use our common sense in everything that we do for a better and peaceful world.

I've also learned that Georges and Sister Rose where already secretly divorced seven months prior to her death. I want to make it clear to everybody that Georges and Sherwin were not the only people who caused Sister Rose to pass away, but some fake pastors in Orlando who didn't want Sister Rose to build her ministry next to theirs also participated indirectly in her death. They said that if they let something like that happen, everybody in their church will leave them and go with Sister Rose, and they won't have anybody left in their ministries. Those fake pastors hate her, and they were very jealous of her to a point where they participated in using black magic against her in a food that they gave to a sister of the church to give to Sister Rose. The minute she finished eating the food, she had a stomachache and diarrhea for more than three days which she talked about in a video on YouTube because they are Freemasons, not pastors. I want the world to know and understand that not every Freemason are bad people. Some choose to do wrong to others, and some chose to do good. This is not the first time it happens. Sister Rose is not the only person. It's going to happen to, and it will continue to happen to many innocent women around the globe who will always try to protect their names, their status or reputation by acting like everything is fine or great. If there are any other women or so-called pastors' wives that find themselves in that same situation, it would be wise to come forward and seek for help before it's too late.

I want all women out there to know that their life is precious and must do everything and anything to preserve it, and stay alive until God says otherwise. Please don't be trapped in a violent or an abusive relationship or marriage by shame, confusion, or blaming yourself when you're not at fault. The only thing you should worry about is your safety and your life. If you find yourself in an abusive relationship or marriage, know the followings:

- You deserve to be treated with dignity and respect.
- You should seek for help.
- You deserve to be happy and safe.
- It's not your fault. You're not to be blamed!
- You deserve true love.

To all men out there who are in a relationship or marriage who don't know that their women are half of them and they're half of their women, let me tell you something, you can't treat your women in any kind of way. Women are queens and princesses. You treat them for who they are, and you automatically become kings. But if you treat them like trash, you're nothing else but the trash cans. That's a fact.

Brothers and sisters, the World Health Organization had confirmed that 30 percent of women worldwide have experienced physical or sexual violence by their intimate partner. And the Center for Disease Control had also released their statistic that revealed that 32.9 percent of women in the United States have experienced physical or sexual violence by their intimate partner. The persons who are supposed to take care and cherish these women are the same men who are violating their rights and mistreating them. How this even possible? Most women around the world would love to have a perfect family and don't want to divide their family, but they do want the violence to STOP completely and don't know what to do and how to do it. All the women that are victims of domestic violence around the world are going through the same thing. It's a common problem among them. Those women refuse to press charges against their abusive partner or husband because they don't want them to go to jail, and when I dig a little bit deeper why such attitudes and behaviors from those victims' part, I found out the following:

- First and foremost, those mothers don't want the father of their children to be in jail, and they are responsible.

- Secondly, they don't want their children to grow up and find that their own mother was the cause of their father's incarceration.
- Thirdly, they don't want their children to grow up with such sticker on their back "their father was a prisoner."
- And lastly, those women need the fathers' support, physically and economically so their children can be in the right side of life, which makes a lot of sense but at the same time can put their lives in extreme danger, and it can cost them their lives because some abusers are very dangerous.

These offenders know those women's weak point which put these women in a very bad position. These abusers rely on things like that so they can keep doing what they do best. Please don't take domestic violence lightly. Many victims didn't have the chance to see their daughters, brothers, sisters, children, and grandchildren growing up, losing their lives in domestic violence. They have no souvenir whatsoever of these family members (lost souvenirs). In the state of mind of most men, they have a mentality thinking that women should be summative to them for one reason or the other. Some even think it's the law. And that's not the case at all, it should be 50/50 in a relationship or marriage. Wherever there's a strong and successful man, there's a woman behind curtains that's pushing and directing such man, believe it or not. So real men understand that women play a major role in who they are and who they become. When it comes to domestic violence, some women chose to stay silent and others looked for help by protesting, yelling, talking to the press, friends, coworkers, family members, organizations. They even organized events on domestic violence, which is a very good thing.

When it comes to some men, they refuse to talk about such nightmare or bring their help when it's needed. They act in such negative way simply because they know that they're the center of such nightmare. It's a men's issue so they are the cause of domestic violence. And that's exactly why we act like it's not our problem and concern. All men in general should take their responsibility or play their part as men when it comes to domestic violence. It's a world pandemic that many women are losing their lives upon. It's an anomaly that concerns each and every man around the world no matter their race, ethnic group, religions, sex, and belief, etc. We must be part of the solution, not part of the problem, and we have, as obligation, to clean our mess and commit ourselves to eradicate "domestic violence" for good, which is a nightmare for most women, while engaging ourselves as real men by organizing events and educating and training others on domestic violence. Each and every citizen in a society has their role to play when it comes to domestic violence. Let's communicate about it more. It's extremely important.

As human beings, we are entitled 100 percent right of our thinking, actions, mind, and life. So being happy and healthy is on us. We decide if we're going to be happy or sad, healthy or unhealthy. We also choose who's going to be our friends and who's not. We choose with whom we are going to spend the rest of our lives. Sometimes we make the right choice, and sometimes we don't and end up paying the price. How would anybody know that person they fall in love with, their companion, their lover, their honey, their sweetheart would one day turn against them and became their worst enemy, the same one who used to care for them, cherish them, be there for them, and who used to tell them how beautiful they are. They're the same ones who are telling them how ugly, worthless, stupid, and dumb that they're now and start abusing them at the same time, kicking, pushing, and killing these women they fall in love with. What motivates these men all of the sudden to cultivate such attitudes and behaviors? Well, such question is not easy at all. The only answer that I can give is that first and foremost, financial stability plays a big role into that equation (no money, no love). Secondly, some people are very sick without you realizing it until it's too late.

Domestic violence is not a jerk. t's a matter of life and death. When you find yourself in so much violence in a daily basic or in an unpredictable way, it will drain you out. It makes you mentally and physically exhausted. It sucks your juice and lets you dry. Your lives are on the line. You need help, and the best bet is to seek for some. It's better to be safe than sorry. Know yourselves, know you're smart, beautiful, not ugly, worthy, not worthless. Therefore, take control of your lives. Do what's best for you so you can live your lives to the fullest. Be blessed, and God has his eyes on you.

Domestic Violence on Children

Brothers and sisters, the same way that "domestic violence" can harm adults psychologically, emotionally, and physically, it can also harm children as well. It can even have some terrible effects on a child's physical development. It also has side effects on the child's learning, become a drug user and an alcoholic, can become very violent, stressed and depressed, and grow up to become killer and can become very unstable. The health and happiness of a youth or a child that's expose to domestic violence are at stake around the world. It has negative impact and affects their developmental growth. Some of these children grow up with no love in their hearts and don't care about anybody not even themselves. It looks like they have no feelings whatsoever. Others create their own little world (isolation). They have no friends because of loneliness. They're clueless of what is acceptable or not, and they're so confused. They sleep and wake up with "domestic violence." They witness and live it day by day either by a drunkard and crackhead father and mother; sometimes it can be an uncle or an Aunt or by adopted parents or caregivers. The number of children, including youth that are witnessing or abusing around the world by domestic violence, is very significant. Such negative situation puts these children in a lot of pain and suffering throughout their lives. The US Department of Justice defines domestic violence as "a pattern of abusive behavior in any relationship that's used by one partner to gain or maintain power or control over another intimate partner."

A lot of parents think that their arguments and fights don't affect their children in any way, big mistake; you better think again. These kinds of parents don't understand that violence and conflict in a family affect the children considerably. And such negative behavior from parents can and will raise the bar for children to develop serious behavioral and emotional problems. And the worse of all this is that not every parents or abusers know or recognize these symptoms. As a result, the children or teens don't get the attention or help that they deserve. Be aware, where domestic violence takes place, children abused follow. In this big square of domestic violence, children do get hurt accidentally or voluntarily. Thereof, their health and safety are at stake.

Symptoms that children may suffer when exposed to domestic violence.

- Children may become extremely aggressive.
- Children may create their own little world (loneliness).
- May see increase or decrease in appetite.
- Hate things that they use to love once.
- Lost interest in education, friends, and fun becomes weird to them.
- Children will become very stressed and depressed.
- Children will be sleepless or sleep more.
- Children will become angry and emotional.
- Children's fear or anxiety will increase.

Children developing these symptoms shouldn't be taken for granted. They should immediately be evaluated by a mental health professional; your children are not safe. They need help ASAP. Domestic violence comes and goes. It acts like a ghost. It will never go away for good. It will come when least expected; therefore, always have a plan B such as a place to go. It doesn't matter, it can be a friend's house or a relative's place. Be prepared for the worse. You can also go to www.thehotline.org for help or call the previous number that I gave in the book. And I want everybody to know that according to experts, many factors are in play, and they influence each and every child's responses to domestic violence differently because it doesn't affect all children the same way. Some of the victims don't really show some obvious symptoms of depression, stress, or have developed their own strategies to deal with the problem. Some may be beaten down by it. For example, let say that two sisters have witnessed their aunt beaten down by their drunk husband and run home to the same scenario where they find their mother lying down on the floor in her blood, just beaten by their father. Certainly, they won't take it the same, and they won't have the same reaction at all.

- When you compare those two, one can feel very sad about what the aunt had to go through, and the other might not care at all and keep doing what he/she was doing.
- The one who acted like he/she doesn't care to what happened to the aunt will act differently finding the mother the way she was. The child is going to be scared by thinking there's a possibility that the mother may die and that quickly can put the child into a stress and depression mood.
- The other might have a totally different way or reaction to what have happened to her mother. Again, it doesn't affect all children the same way.

Children are meant to be protected. Please keep your violence to yourselves. They don't need to be a witness or victims of such nightmare. God gives them to us so we can take good care of them and make them feel safe. We will have questions to answer before God for the attitudes and behaviors that we had toward them. Never forget that God's in control.

The Impact of Domestic Violence on Children

Unfortunately, children are victims of domestic violence (directly or indirectly). What happened between the adults in the household follow them through their lifetime unfortunately. Parents who argue and fight in front of their children also abuse their children believe it or not. Things that I had witness, children wake up in the middle of the night and hear their mothers pleading for their lives by begging the offender, "Please stop, I beg you, don't kill me," or seeing the mother with their own eyes lying on the floor in her blood that's everywhere. And when they see what the abuser had done to their moms, they immediately drop to a deep sadness. Some will beg their dads not to kill their mothers; and others will attack, push, and punch, even kill their fathers, just to save their mothers. Also others will pull a knife or a gun on the abusers, that happened to be their fathers, just to make sure that their mothers are safe. Some of them will stab or shoot without a second thought just because they're tired of what their mothers have to go through day by day or maybe too scared that their father might kill their mothers, and they don't want that; therefore, they will do anything to STOP him. Sometimes, some children who tried to protect their mothers also get abused physically or even got killed by their fathers or the other way around. Most abusers have restraining orders against them but still break in the homes of their ex-girlfriends or ex-wives so they can keep doing what they do best, abuse them.

A restraining order for those who don't know is "a temporary court order issued to prohibit an individual from carrying out a particular action, especially approaching or contacting a specified person." In other words, it's a court order that limits the abuser from going near the victim or a piece of paper that protects the victim. When the negative attitudes and behaviors of the offenders make surface, it destroys the children like a big wave, and it really puts them in a very awkward situation in life. It's a terrifying nightmare that will take them a while to wake up from. It's possible that the abusers can be arrested and be thrown in jail for attempted murder; but guess what, the fear will always be in the children, and they will always be scared and don't feel safe because the memory of the past will hunt them forever if they don't give them the attention and help that they deserve. Even though the fathers are in jail or dead, some children still wake up in the middle of the night and run to their mothers' room and wake them up and ask them, "Are you okay, Mom?" And when the mother says, "Yes, honey, I am," that's when they feel a little bit better. The reason why the children act the way they do is because they're in a fear mood that makes them think that it might happen again. Therefore, they stay in a state of mind of being scared and afraid that brings those worries and instability. And that's exactly the mood that they find themselves in when they become more aggressive, violent, and destructible. Such negative vibe gives them a change of behavior where they meet with stress, depression, and loneliness. They also have some changes in their sleep where they suffer from insomnia (trouble "sleeping) or, if falling asleep for few minutes, having constant nightmare of the past (PTSD). Some kids choose to talk about it, but others choose to keep it to themselves. Those who chose not to talk about it are in greater danger than those who choose to talk about it (meaning, they will need more attention, love, and help that they can get to wake them up from such nightmare). Counseling is extremely important for them to do better. The sad part is that most of these children don't like night time. In their state of mind, they know it will be soon time for them to go to bed where they will dream about what they and their moms went through which turn into nightmares and make them hate night time. They also hear noises where there's none. They see their fathers as monsters who want to swallow in whole their families and always think that these monsters will come to get them and their mothers; that's living in constant nightmares.

Some children still want to maintain a relationship with their fathers but some don't simply because they're scared of them for what they put them through. They're scared that the father might end up hurting them or even kill them, and that's exactly why they want to stay away from their fathers. These are things that need to be fix. These fathers need to do better so their children can be in their lives. Each and every child deserve their father in their lives so they can have a real man to look up to, a real role model.

Mothers that went through such nightmare with their children and raising them alone need to talk to their children and let them know that what have happened is the past, and they're safe now, and it will never reproduce itself again. Let them know that having bad dreams is part of sleeping, but it's not real. It's just having a dream, and there's no reason to be afraid and scared (I love you, and I will take good care of you, and I promise it will never happen again) by saying that you will build some solid ground for your children to stand on knowing that there's no earthquake that can destroy it, talking to them make them believe that they are really safe and their mothers love them very much, hugging and kissing them from time to time (they need love and attention more than ever before). And make sure you teach them about God, and you take them to church so God can make them better people with a safe future. Remember that the Lord has his eyes on you and the children. He loves you for ever and ever.

Domestic Violence on Pregnant Women

Experts say, "Adding pregnancy to an already violently relationship sometimes things can get worst" (when you're pregnant in a relationship or marriage and your partner who's supposed to love you and take good care of you and finds you once as the most beautiful woman on the planet earth is now calling you all kinds of names, throwing objects at you while you're pregnant to hurt you and your baby that you're carrying for him, he even calls you ugly whenever he wants to). It's hard to believe, but it's the reality. People do change for the better or worst. That's what we need to understand. People don't stay the same, and we do change.

Experts say, "If you're in an abusive relationship, there're two things to consider and that can't be ignored, conditions can be worsen and the violence will intensify."

- When you leave!
- When you're pregnant!

So unfair to those women who are carrying those offenders' babies. Those abusers force them to do hard work that they're not supposed to do while pregnant. Those men also abuse them physically, emotionally, and mentally. Those women don't deserve to be treated like that, and I know that a lot are happening to those women behind closed doors, things that they would never imagine that would happen to them such as name-calling, beatings, kicking, false accusations, punching, yelling, intimidations, and hard work while pregnant make them feel like they're not wanted and loved. If something like this is happening to you, know that you're in the dark side of life so get out now and take your first step to see the other side which is the light side by seeking for help because they're many people and organizations that can help you. It's worth it to help someone that you know or don't know that's in a violent relationship by saying or doing something, help save a life before it is too late.

It's never okay for any man to put his hands on a woman pregnant or not only cowards do that. The reason why I love and respect all women, especially my wife, is because I had a mother who carried me in her belly for nine months and breastfed me for two years, cleaned and changed me when I needed to, and made sure that I was safe at all times and took good care of me.

So when I think of these things, it gives me the right attitude toward women and make me the kind of person that I am today. Most men who are abusing women were also abused or didn't raise by anybody at all. They raise themselves. Therefore, they think that it's okay to mistreat and abuse their loved ones. It's a worldwide pandemic that's destroying many families, including the abusers themselves. One out of ten women experience "domestic violence" doing pregnancy, and be aware that they're not the only one experiencing the violence and the abuse. The children that they're carrying also went through this nonsense. There are two victims when violence occurs while pregnant. The mother is at serious risk while carrying the baby. Depression, stress, anxiety, and injuries even death is possible! The enfant is at risk of any kind of injuries, premature growth, and miscarriage, etc.

Pregnancy in a violent marriage or relationship can be very dangerous at time of dependency, isolation, anger, discrimination, accusations, addictions, hostility, name-calling, emotional, depression, stress, anxiety, and financial difficulties. Such nightmares doing pregnancy can lead to conflict. Any woman in such situation can be very vulnerable. Every nine seconds on a watch, a phone, or a clock, a woman is insulted in the United States of America and around the world. Domestic violence happens in all fifty states of America where women got stabbed, kicked, punched, shot, and killed. It's something that each and every concerned citizen should take seriously and bring to the table their participation to change the situation. Be part of the solution, not the problem.

The biggest mistake that some women are committing is telling their men that they are leaving them, and they don't have anything to do with them. It's a big mistake that kills many women worldwide. They don't understand by telling their men that they are leaving can push them into a jealousy that will awaken their rage that might cause them their lives, just like it costs Tareeka Jones and her sister theirs. Tareeka Jones was a devoted mother of three young girls. Kevin Tyrice, former boyfriend of Tareeka, who was also the father of her third baby girl killed both sisters Tareeka Jones and her sister Jalisa Walls-Harris while two of the girls were watching—what a tragedy, may they rest in peace. This monster destroyed a beautiful family just because of his rage that he couldn't control when he was told by Tareeka Jones that she's going to leave him.

They're not the first, and they will not be the last unfortunately. Many mothers and babies worldwide are dead during delivery or while the mothers are giving birth due to extreme violence and abused during pregnancy which is very sad and unfortunate. There's also a serious risk of suicide and suicide attempts during pregnancy. All pregnant women around the world who are in abusive relationships or marriages need to understand that it's not their fault, and it will never be. They're just innocent victims. My question to you is how can it be your fault when you're the victims? Just start asking yourselves that question before you start blaming yourselves, okay? Just be fair to yourselves. You deserve that much. Some of these abusers choose to use violence against their partners or wives because they're jealous of their own babies. You might say, what is he talking about? Hold it, I'm not losing it, not just yet. I say it's a form of jealousy from the abusers' side because they feel as though that their partners or wives who are carrying their babies are giving or paying more attention to the babies than them and become very angry at the mother and let their temper control them and turn them into violent and abusive individuals and do the worse that anybody could have imagined.

Here are ten components of Vautoir's wall of good intentions that can cause a man to abuse his wife or partner that I'm sharing with you.

- Jealousy can come from different angle.
- Being broke.
- Love to be in control.
- Unwanted pregnancy.
- Can't meet his expectations.
- Having an affair.
- Hardship.
- Being a substance user.
- Being an alcoholic!
- When love is no more.

Victim or abusive women globally deserve a break that they don't have to beg for, so may the lawmakers let their common sense into play. May the love and protections of the Almighty be with all women around the world, and may the Holy Spirit be with them forever and ever.

I want everybody to understand that whatever problem that somebody wants to solve. Violence is not the answer, and it will never be because violence breeds violence. When your partner or wife is pregnant, it should be the best moment of your life. The person that you love is carrying your child; therefore, you should be happy and excited. It's a must to treat your woman with respect, love, and dignity, pregnant or not. But it's essential that you protect her during the pregnancy. Protecting her is also protecting the baby. Both of them deserve your protection; they should be your first priority. A real father that loves his family always want peace and love to display in the house and throughout their lives. Love is not a game. Either you love to be loved, or you find yourself a corner to go and sit down because you don't know what love is, and you're not ready to commit.

Dating Online

Many women put their children's and their lives in great danger by going online to find a lover or someone to spend the rest of their lives with. I know nowadays the internet is the fastest and most popular way to find a partner or a friend with benefits, someone you can share all your secret and love with. Trust and believe, finding love online is very risky and dangerous, and it can put you in harm's way, even cost you and your children's lives if you have any. Most criminals or abusers are online too searching for love. You don't know who's who. You're just taking a chance but a chance that can costs you big time. This kind of love has no other name but dangerous love. I have to say also that some people do find true love online. But trust me, it's a very risky decision; and the percentage is very low, very poor decision when you just meet with the person, and all of the sudden, you choose to move together with a complete stranger someone you don't really know or don't take any time to get to know that person and a poor decision can be very fatal sometimes. Many women are desperate for love so they find online dating as a great opportunity. Never take time to ask themselves valuable questions such as,

- What if he's an abuser?
- What if he's a rapist?
- What if he doesn't like children?
- What if he's crazy?
- What if he's a thief?

These are the important and valuable questions that any woman who uses her common sense should ask herself before dating any stranger online just to keep herself and her children safe. The best way for anybody to fall in love is to fall in love with someone you grow up with or you know enough for a while or you know from your school. If it's not the case for you, well, get to know the person very well before you say this beautiful word *yes*. It's way much safer than dealing with a complete stranger; love who you know and those who love you. Some people are so abusive and violent they will stab and shoot you like it's nothing with no remorse. And that's exactly why you should never fall in love with a complete stranger, and that's what I call "good judgement." Some criminals are very charming and good looking, and some of them always keep a smile on their faces but don't have a kind heart, but a "lion heart." That's why no woman should fall in love with a man because of his beautiful eyes, smile, or good looks. I sometimes overheard women saying to themselves or friends, "Oh my god, he is so handsome. I would love to have a baby by him." These women don't use their common sense, especially the young adults, so it's very easy for them to put their lives in danger.

Men and women who use their common sense or their awareness, which allows them to communicate with themselves, don't see the outside beauty but the inside one, and that's the only way that we can see the light that's shining in our partner or spouse (true and lasting love). Not all men are ready to commit in a relationship. Their lack of kindness, compassion, understanding, and respect don't allow them to be. These women don't understand that when they open their doors to these kinds of men, they just dig their own hole and bury themselves alive unfortunately. My advice to anyone that's falling in love is always look for the inside qualities than the outside ones because the outside ones can play you for a fool.

CHAPTER 5

How to Love and Be Loved

Anyone who wants to be loved, the first thing to do is to love God, yourself, and other people. Without this important concept, love will be lost, and you will never be able to find it. "Whatever we want others to do to us, we do to them." That's exactly what you call "reproduction." We want others to love us. We should love them first, and then they will love us back. We want people to treat us right, respect us. We set the example so they can follow because what goes around comes around.

Statistics have proven that many of us who are after love are not ready to love or to be loved. And as we all know, we are living in a world full of toxic people unfortunately who lay a lot of toxic eggs in marriages and relationships around the world just because they are not ready to commit and have no clue what love is really about. Very seldom they face with the reality of the effort, the time, the investment, and the work that relationships and marriages require. They require self-work and teamwork; our personal effort as a couple has to launch first from my end and yours before we can think about teamwork. I make an effort to love you, to cherish you, to respect you, to care about you, to understand you, to treat you with compassion, and to be kind to you, etc. As my partner or my spouse, you have to reproduce the same effort so we can move up to the teamwork and meet true love so we can accomplish greatness in togetherness. I strongly believe that a lot of young men out there have very poor example and understanding of what love, marriages, and relationships are all about. Growing up in an abusive and violent family, seeing their abusive dads beating, kicking, punching, yelling, stabbing, and shooting their mothers right before their eyes make them grow up with doubts and misbeliefs in their hearts when it comes to love, marriages, and relationships. To these young men, I am telling you today, that's not the way it works; this negative behavior of your fathers have nothing to do with love. They acted the way they acted for three reasons:

- Understand rather that your fathers are sick individuals who need help.
- Probably didn't have fathers to teach them how to treat women.
- Maybe they didn't know any better.

You are different from your dads; therefore, you don't have to treat any women the way you fathers did your moms. You can be different. Do your best to make your girlfriends or wives proud of you for the way you communicate and treat them. No human being deserves to be mistreated and abused, especially someone you love and care about. It pays to be unique on your own way. It's more than okay to be different. Think positively, stay positive, and act positively so you can make a difference in your lives and other people in your surroundings. It will show people that you're wise men because by looking at your fathers' poor examples, you didn't let it affect you in a negative way; rather, you found a way to pull away from it. By looking at your parents' way of living, you separate the negative from the positive and take this positivity into your own lives and build your own family, that's smart. You have learned to treat your children and women differently so you can grow and strive together; you have risen where your parents have failed. If you're not smart enough to see or understand it the way you should, you will fall into the same cycle as your fathers.

It's possible that in your hearts and minds, you would like to have an awesome, happy, and healthy relationships and marriages;

but in your subconscious, you will find yourself reproducing the same dilemma as your fathers. It's really unfair to bring innocent women that can truly love you into your miserable life. Falling in love is a natural and necessary part of life. God created us to fall in love and form bonds with each other. As human beings, we have a lack of love, and it seems like it's almost impossible to find true love for most of us. We are smart. We are business people, doctors, engineers, nurses, lawyers, actors, CEOs, singers, authors, etc. Unfortunately, we feel lonely with no one to love and to love us. And most of us refuse to understand that the real love that we are missing comes from God who gave us his only son to be our savior. By neglecting his son, Jesus Christ, we are neglecting the love we need and want. We write, sing, and listen to a lot of great songs about love, yet we're still crawling like a baby when it comes to love. True love is the bleach that washes away all stains such as violence, abuse, hate, anger, jealousy, pain, and suffering, broken heart, accusations, and blames. It gives us a clear understanding and vision on sharing, giving, carrying, humility, generosity, sympathy, loyalty, honesty, mercy, kindness, forgiveness, respect, gratitude, compassion, and grace. So as we all know and understand, when we wash and bleach our dirty laundry, they become clean and fresh (meaning we get rid of the stains and dirt). It's the same thing with love, and there's no difference. It is time for us as children of God to start giving the real meaning to love by washing and bleaching our dirty laundry.

Love is the most popular word. It's known internationally. Each and every human being wants and needs love, and yet no single one of us have the right understanding of what love really is. That's why most of us replace it by money when we know damn well money doesn't by happiness. It can only buy you material things. We can make our best to make someone smile, feel appreciated, wanted, important, needed, and feel good about himself or herself but still you cannot make a person happy. It's something that's completely and totally out of our jurisdiction. Unfortunately, some of us see love as a transaction. "Give me what I want and need, take good care of me, and then I will love you." This is not love. It's just an exchange for desire and pleasure. As long as you can fulfill my needs and wants, you are the one that I'm looking for which sometimes lead to disappointment, anger, frustration, and isolation. Love is also a May flower that needs proper care, nourish it with water and the right seed so it can grow and blossom. If we give the same treatment to love, we will give it a chance to grow to what God created it to be without forcing it or turning it into something else or give it our own meaning. By giving love a chance to show what it's about, that's true love, and anything other than that is not love. You can call it what you want, feel free, but love.

Love is also about the followings:

- *Loyalty*
    Loyalty is being devoted and faithful to your partner or your spouse, a true lover that's loyal, reliable, and will never let you down (a two-way street).
- *Obedience*
    Obedience is when two lovers comply with each other's request. It's the law of submission. We obey each other. And whenever there's a disagreement, we communicate or discuss it peacefully.
- *Values*
    It's when in a relationship or marriage, each spouse or partner value each other. They show one another that they are important, worthy, wanted, and needed.
- *Enjoyable*
    *E*njoyable is to demonstrate your love for your spouse or your partner with no hold back or feeling any shame so you can make him or her feel good and loved.

If we give love its real meaning and use it the right way, it will help others by making sure that they suffer and struggle less; it would transform their miserable and poor lives into hope. Too many homeless, hungry people, and hatred in this world because of ignorance and selfishness of others. When you love someone, you want that person to smile and be there for that person. But why hurt that same person you claim to love? Each and every one of us have our own definition of the word *love*. Many of us think the real love is the one that we see in the movies, drama shows, comedies, and Facebook; they are nothing else but fake love. And walking with our eyes closed, we will fall into the trap of pain and suffering because in reality, these ideas are nothing but fairytales. It's just a kind of love that is tied to a living-room table that you will not be able to use at your convenience because there's no true pleasure and happiness in such love.

And when the love is based on ownership and selfishness, it will be followed by pain and suffering, and heartbreak will be inevitable. For example, when someone says, "I'll buy you whatever you want. I'll take good care of you if you decide to be mine." That's not love. It's a possessive type of love. And such love is so fake that it carries with it all the pain and suffering around the world either way you look at it. True love is not about money or what I can do for you. It comes from the heart and the heart alone. If I ask this question to anybody—who's the person you hate the most—even though we have no right to hate but we still do it anyway, most people would say with no hesitation their EX. And these are people who used to kiss, play, hug each other from time to time, have children and hold hands, now holding grudges against each other, even hold guns and knives at each other's head out of selfishness, hatred, jealousy, and obsession. These are couples who used to share tender kisses and had great affection for one another, and all of the sudden, they feel hatred for each other. My question is, was there any love there in the first place? I would say maybe, maybe not, because there's a possibility that they were in love and they ended up hating each other depending of the circumstances and what they put each other through. Or maybe there wasn't any love at all. It was just interest (love of interest or love with benefit).

That's also what you call a cycle of pain and pleasure that most of us went through; it's all about sex. It makes us feel alive just like cocaine, heroin, and other drugs that addicts take to get high in a state of mind that the drugs will take their problems away without knowing that when the high goes away, they will come back to their pain and suffering. The problems go away when you're high because you don't think about them, but the minute that you return to normal, the first thing you will face and see are your problems that you thought you were hiding from.

I truly believe that it's time for us to wake up as human beings when it comes to love. The time has come for us to strive for a higher form of love. The ideal that one person will satisfy all of our needs and wants is very unfair and selfish. Thinking and depending on someone else to fix all your problems or you can bring solutions to everybody's problems is poor thinking or poor judgement. What you need to do is to learn to love and communicate with yourself first so you can love others unconditionally. When you are able to take care of your emotional needs and love yourself for who you really are, then you will be able to do the same for others. That's accepting others for who they are because you already accept yourself for who you are. It's a bad judgement to see others for what they're not or to force them to look and act like somebody else. Learn to love and accept your partner, your spouse, your family member, your coworkers, and friends for who they are and what God created them to be, not what you want them to be or how you see them. And that's exactly where true love is hiding, and you can discover it by applying such positive attitude and behavior. We have to learn to love and appreciate each other no matter the differences (skin color, religion, beliefs, and ethnic groups); we are brothers and sisters created by one God and one blood. Please don't let selfishness, greed, and ignorance destroy such beautiful family that God puts together so we can live in love, harmony, and peace that we deserve. The type of love we need and that will change the way we see our partners and spouses is a love where there will be no anger and there will only be kindness, respect, understanding, compassion, tenderness, acceptance, and full of humility. That's the kind of love I am looking forward to spread around the world so in togetherness, we can save marriages and relationships for the well-being of the children. You will be able to do other things with your time instead of chasing love by becoming an instrument of love. You can be a violin, a guitar, or else that will play a nice note in the ears of your partner or spouse that will leave them with a smile on their faces and hearts that will drop them right on the path of happiness and stay healthy for life. In reality, when you have such attitude, you don't have to seek for love. It will find you. It's a wonderful thing when two people are in a romantic relationship understand and respect one another. It's an attitude that each and every individual should strive for because it's rare and awesome. If you don't know how to love, you will sooner or later destroy such a beautiful word, even end up hurting people you love and others. You're nothing but a mechanic without the proper tools who will end up damaging the part or hurting his hands.

True Love

True love is an unbreakable and inseparable commitment. It's strong and pure. It's a feeling that runs deeper into someone's heart than physical attraction. Most men fall in love because the women are beautiful (physical appearance). They close the door on the inside beauty, which is the most important aspect in a relationship. All they see and can think of is the beautiful body (nice butt.) What they don't know is that the inside beauty is way much greater than the outside beauty. I would rather fall in love with an ugly woman from outside who is beautiful inside than falling in love with a beautiful woman from the outside and ugly from the inside (common sense). But some people do find women that are beautiful outside and inside, which is a blessing. Also others fall in love with women who are ugly outside and inside, whom they call the "beasts." It's the same for women. Most of them always look for handsome men from the outside and very ugly inside (monsters). My point is that someone can be very ugly outside and beautiful in the inside. Also they can be very beautiful outside and very ugly inside. The inside beauty lets you know exactly what kind of a person that you're dealing with. It will let you know if you're dealing with a good or evil person. Therefore, be very careful with whom you are falling in love with. Be aware that those you consider ugly men or women can be the most beautiful people ever (sweet, gentle, respectful, compassionate, loyal, kind, and really know how to love. Those you consider as beautiful because of their look can be very evil, disrespectful, full of hatred, and anger, emotional, disloyal, savage, unkind, cheaters, or a "monster in action." At the same time, some people are beautiful inside out, so they possess both qualities, which is wonderful but very rare. For me personally, being gorgeous or attractive is the beauty that person has inside just like my wife Yvonie. She has a distinctive personality. She's always smiling and can laugh at almost anything. She keeps me healthy because she makes me smile at all times; and when she makes me smile, my heart smiles. And when my heart smiles, I stay healthy, and that's why I love her so much. She is a woman that makes me very happy and feel good about myself. We are inseparable, very kind and caring person.

A beautiful woman is someone who shows her inside beauty wherever she goes and in any circumstances that may occur, a person who is kind and cares about other people, a woman who knows how to value love and have the ability not to make life complicated, a woman that a husband, a boyfriend, her surrounding, someone that children and adults can trust and rely on when they need her the most, a woman that everybody feels as though they never have enough of and at the same time makes you believe that your life matters. What I really want to share with my readers is that no matter how sexy a woman looks and have the nicest body and face ever doesn't make her beautiful. It's not about how she looks, makeup she wears, what she put on, or the way she combs her hair. It's about her smile, her body language, the warmth that she brings to people around her, and the way she treats or interacts with others; that's the beauty to look for (and when you understand that you become a very smart person who's after nothing else but true love), a beauty that will catch both your eyes and heart. A feeling that will bring you happiness and joy and makes you want to be with her or next to her at all times. She makes you laugh when you're with her and sad when you are not like you are missing half of you. Beauty has nothing to do with appearance but quality, and when you think like that, you will fall right in the basket of true love.

A beautiful woman is also someone with a kind heart, a person that can forgive anybody and can make anybody's heart beat faster with her kindness and love, when smiling can leave some sparkles behind and when seen will leave you thinking about pure perfection. Certainly, that's a beauty that will attract whoever wherever, someone that's different on every angle than everybody else, and believe me, that's exactly when true love finds you and grabs your heart. Someone that says yes to almost everything, things that most people would say no to, she says yes, she's someone with a golden heart. Everybody's problem is her problem.

What she can do to anyone:

- She has the ability to take your breath away by spreading love, compassion, respect, and understanding wherever she goes and in everything that she's doing.
- She also can make people unable to think, forget how to behave properly, etc.

It's all about her generosity, attitude, and behavior, a woman that completes you. I call that a "blossom love" that will blow you away. That's a gorgeous woman, don't you think? A compassionate woman that shares your deepest personal views and that shows understanding, also a woman that you hug and never let go and would like to get stack with on a good kiss. A woman because of who she is inside is showing on the outside and cover both of you with glory and beauty, a beautiful woman that's unique and doesn't need to fit in while being her own person, a woman who doesn't care about what others think about her by being herself, a woman who really knows how to make her lover or her husband or others feel good about themselves no matter what the circumstances may be, a woman that's not very attractive but have the ability to make anyone's heart melt. That's unique and different, isn't it? That's the kind of woman that every true man dreams to have, a woman that can make your life beautiful, an understandable and compassionate woman, which will bring positive change into your life for good.

Most men around the world unfortunately gave a whole different meaning to the word *beautiful*. For them, it means a woman with big butt and large breasts which is false. They never think about the inside beauty quality of the person. They are blind in that sense.

They have no clue of what true love really is. They always have the wrong perspective about love and women in general.

To all men out there who really want to know how to love, and be loved, here are thirty components of Vautoir's wall of good intentions that I am sharing with you.

- Don't be selfish. Mine is yours, and yours is mine, especially when it comes to money!
- Do not judge.
- Accept the person for who she is. Love me or love me not!
- Make sure to keep your partner or spouse happy!
- Do the laundry and wash the dishes from time to time.
- Help your lover in any way that you can so you can grow and strive together.
- Do not accuse with no tangible proof.
- Let her know how much you love and appreciate her.
- Always leave her a thank-you note.
- Call her from work and tell her how much you miss her.
- Always be kind and gentle to the woman that you love.
- Cry with her when she's crying.
- Laugh with her when she's laughing.
- When she's sad, do anything in your power to make her laugh.
- Practice forgiveness, always!
- Value her and her family.
- Communicate with her, it's a must!
- Always tell her the truth!
- Be honest and loyal to her.
- Do not cheat.
- Show her that you believe in her.
- Never STOP reminding her how beautiful she is.
- Make her goals and her dreams yours. Take it personal.
- Surprise her from time to time with something that she likes.
- Take her to places that she loves.
- Spend some quality time together.

- Always protect and ready to defend her in any circumstances.
- Be willing to do anything for her.
- Be there for her when she needs you the most.
- Ensure her that you guys are meant for each other.

Love is a positive and good thing because everybody wants it and after it. It's a feeling that everyone wants to explore. It will be very difficult, almost impossible, to really love someone without any understanding of the true nature or meaning of love and how to define it. For a word with such great importance, we should understand it better.

When you love someone, it requires a lot of efforts. It's a very emotional feeling that requires investment such as time, understanding, compassion, and respect. It also comes along with anger, hate, conflict, stress, depression, etc. Love is a risk, but a risk that each and every one of us has to take because we all are in need of such risk, a risk that we can turn into positivity. Be aware, a positive state of mind is above all. Love is also an addiction. When you're in love, you become addicted to the presence of the person that you love (can't live without that person, can't eat, can't sleep, and can't wait for tomorrow to come so you can see that person again). It's an ongoing excitement that comes with a flame that no water can put out, and that's loving and missing that person terribly.

Expressing Your Love

To express your love for a woman that you love and cherish is through gifts and flowers. Believe me, women love flowers and gifts. They find it very romantic, and they love it. It's also a way to show your affection toward them. When you go out with them, it doesn't matter how many people are there; act like it's just the two of you, and nobody else is around. Give your lady your full undivided attention. She deserves it. Remember now that women are princesses and queens, and by any means necessary, they have to be treated for who they are and what they represent. See them like your own mothers because a good man always treats his woman the same way he would treat his mother. Make them feel special by turning your phone off and by focusing on them only. Always look at your lover in the eye while communicating with her and go to deep listening when she's talking to you. Help your girl in any way that you can, even if it's out of your reach. Such attitude and behavior will tell her point-blank how much that you love and care about her. Take the time to do for them what they don't like to do, and they won't be able to live without you. They will appreciate you. For example, if she doesn't like to do laundry, do it for her so she doesn't have to think about it or go do it. Practice physical touch. It feels good to be touched by someone that you love. It also promotes good times and good feelings between you two. Kissing, hugging, and holding hands are best suited to show real love.

Love is a two-way street. Both partners or spouses have to put in a lot of time and effort if they want their relationship or marriage successful. In order to straighten your love, you have to feed it every day with the right seed so it can grow and last. Love is not meant to be short. It's forever because it doesn't come with an expiration date. It's not your ID, your passport, or your own life; it's greater than that, understand that.

Forgiveness: The Path of True Love

In all relationships and marriages there are what you call conflicts; therefore, voluntarily or involuntarily, we are hurting each other. Some conflicts leave us with deep wounds and nightmares that we think we will never get rid of or heal from. Other pain and suffering are hash languages and physical attacks on a daily basis. The insults and mistreating force, some of us take some protective measures such as putting some barriers, fight back in any way we possibly can or a court order which, most of the time, don't protect us against our abusers because they don't follow through with it. We are human beings, and we make some mistakes. I made some. My wife made some, and that's why both of us are very grateful for forgiveness; we learn from our mistakes, To forgive and to be forgiven is the path of true love. When you forgive your partner or your spouse for a mistake made, know that you also forgive yourself because sooner or later down the road, you will make a mistake that will need to be forgiven. Then your partner or your spouse will forgive you with no hesitation, that's reproduction.

In a relationship or marriage for some, it's easier to hold on to the past and throw it to your face when an argument occurs than to forgive. They don't understand that a past offense stays a past offense, and with no forgiveness, there will be no progress and no peace in the house. When you choose not to forgive, not only that you are not going to be forgiven neither, but you allow your spouse or partner that made a simple mistake to be stuck with it and not to be free from it. When you act in such negative way, you are not only hurting your partner or your spouse but yourself as well because you will be carrying the pain and suffering, anger, and bitterness with you from the mistake that he or she made with you wherever you go. It's like you choose to drink poison instead of forgiving your lover, big mistake. I've used the word *poison* because when you keep yourself in the past and refuse to forgive, you just open your arms and welcome negativity which is a killer. So it's like drinking poison, a kind that will kill you softly but surely.

When you choose to forgive, it's a conscious decision that you make, and it doesn't mean that the pain and suffering goes away instantly. For the pain and suffering that you cause to your partner or spouse can be devastating; therefore, forgiveness is just a healing process of the damage that you cause. Understand that emotional injuries take longer to heal than physical ones because the impact damages their belief, their happiness, their health, and their success. It's a disaster when you have a feeling that the entire world has collapsed on you. It also like an earthquake that falls on you and finds yourself under the debris. Hurting your partner or your spouse's feeling is not a good thing, and it will never be. It's way much better to cherish and forgive one another for a better family and a peaceful environment. Also such attitude and behavior will prevent your lover from having a trauma that will move to the stage of shock and rage, blame, insecurity, hate, guilt, etc.

Let us practice forgiveness so we can free ourselves and the ones that we love from such nightmare. If we don't allow forgiveness to be the path of our true love, our traumatic hurts and wounds will never be healed or will take longer to heal. Most of us think that the real logic is to hurt back those who hurt us (revenge) because we put the Word of God on the side, which tells us everything that we need to know about forgiveness. We choose revenge over forgiveness when God specifically said, "Leave all revenge to me." For example, if a husband cheats on his wife, she thinks the best thing to do for some is to cheat also. I'm not saying that some have the right to cheat and others don't. All I'm saying is that revenge is not the best solution to your husband's mistake. There is a lot of other different ways that you as the wife can go about. The first and best one is forgiveness because each and every one in life deserve a second chance. I say a second chance, but Jesus Christ our Lord said to forgive repeatedly seventy-seven times seven. That means to forgive the same offense over and over again which is a necessity in marriages and relationships. It doesn't only apply to partners and spouses but to friends, strangers, coworkers, family members, etc. Our Lord instructed us to forgive the multitude of offenses that we are facing day by day by others. As we can see, our savior was strong on forgiveness. It was his ideal teaching. It's an awesome gift that he left for humanity, and that's exactly why forgiving others is mandatory. In my understanding, if there's one thing that can cure this world of fear, anger, hate, violence, bitterness, frustration, stress, disloyal, dishonesty, conflict, war, discomfort, selfishness, destruction, jealousy, envy, greed, and hypocrisy, it's forgiveness. Let say if you have been deeply hurt by your partner or your spouse the one person you have trusted with all your heart, spirit, and mind, in reality, forgiveness would be the last thing in your mind, but you can't see only one side but both because the reward of forgiveness is great.

- It will heal your emotions and take you to the right path.
- It will restore the family's happiness, love, and trust for a better future in which both of you can explore.

- It will give both of you a chance to stay together for the success and well-being of your children.

How can anyone love somebody without forgiveness? True forgiveness is true love that can free you from pain and suffering. When you know how to forgive, you know how to keep "a keeper" and be blessed. I know that forgiveness doesn't walk alone. It has a series of negative emotions that keep it company such as pain and suffering, fear, anger, and bitterness which most of us close our eyes on like they don't exist. Unfortunately, we can't get too far in life without seeing them right behind us, following us. We have been hurt in the past; therefore, we have experienced a lot of pain and suffering and other negative feelings that will transform our current perception of our lovers, along with how we think and act. It will affect nearly every aspect of our lives: health, attitudes, and behaviors and happiness. The best and most important thing is to forgive and let go for our well-being. I know to forgive someone is not easy also to free someone from guilt who has hurt you or wrong you. It's not that simple. Intelligently, the right way to look at it and see it is to have the understanding that it's not about the person that hurts you, but it's about you and only you. It's about you because when you forgive the person who wrong you, you also forgive yourself by releasing yourself to stress, anger, depression, hate, and all other negative feelings you can think of; therefore, you're poison free.

I know that a lot of you have been hurt in the past. Maybe it's time for you to put down the load that you been carrying for so long and take a deep breath and give a ring to forgiveness for your own good. Trust and believe, forgiveness can't replace the pain and suffering that you went through, but it can ease them and keep you going. It's your only out of jail-free card. Ultimately, it's your pass to the path of true love for yourselves, partners, or spouses. It will allow you to feel again the positive feelings you used to feel before you were hurt such as true love, happiness, peace, and joy. When you know how to forgive, you don't only heal your emotional and physical scars but those of your partners and spouses also. Most people who wrong others go to their conscience and their conscience reach to their subconscious and regret everything that they said or done if they have a conscience because some people don't, and that's why they have no remorse when they do wrong. And when they do have a conscience, they find themselves in pain for three reasons:

- They regret that they hurt their partners or wives and show remorse.
- They don't want their love ones to find out what they did so it causes pain.
- Whatever they say wrongly, they didn't mean it because they said it out of anger; therefore, it makes them suffer.

It's very unhealthy to hold on your grudges, resentments, and pain and suffering; the health complications can be very devastating. It can lead to the followings:

- Unhappiness
- High blood pressure
- Unhealthy relationships
- Can feel depressed
- Can become very hostile
- Loneliness
- Very low self-esteem
- Heart complications
- Anxiety
- Negative thinking

When you decide not to forgive and let go, you just give green light to these health complications which I mention above to define your lives and take control of it. And these health complications can only take you to a one-way street (self-destruction). If you don't change the way you think, the way you see and understand things, and the way you react to things, you will never have the ability to change things in your relationships or marriages. If you don't know how to forgive your own family, how in the world you're going to forgive others? Forgiveness is the big brother of kindness so when you don't forgive, it's impossible to be kind to yourselves and others. Do yourselves a favor. Be kind to yourselves and others by forgiving other people. The more you forgive others, the better chance you will have in life to embrace compassion and understanding, the more prepare you will be to welcome change, at the same time to be on the right path, the path of true love. For the people who torture you, lie to you, kill your husbands, wives, members of your family, friends, and coworkers, and for those who put your loved ones in jail or prison while they are innocent, please don't hate them. Instead, forgive them and pray for them so God can change their evil hearts. Trust and believe, it doesn't help at all to hate because it's a word that's full of diseases. If you allow yourselves to hate, you just open your hearts to the enemy, the devil, so he can own your souls. And that's exactly what he wants and after. Be aware that you don't belong to the devil nor here to please him but God. Let the light shine into your heart so you can keep the devil out because he hates the light. And that's exactly why those who are serving him or his children love darkness so much. Be happy with yourselves no matter what life brings. Our Lord had place love into each of us just like an electric wire so we can shock one another with love. Why can't we do just that? It's not that difficult, is it?

Love is the only missile that can be launched to destroy all evil forever; therefore, let us love one another. Remember that love is forgiveness, and forgiveness is love. They are twins. When you know how to love, you automatically become a better person, and at the same time, you cultivate lasting joy and happiness in your life that will take you to your dream ride where you will meet with peace and harmony. Love, to tell you the truth, is a feeling that's different from all other feelings. It's a vital emotion that every human being possesses and can feel. Love and forgiveness are what relationships and marriages really need to grow and strive. Jesus Christ's teaching was all about love. He taught us the importance of forgiveness and love. Yet most people around the world still struggle to love and to forgive others because they have a lack of forgiveness and love of themselves, or maybe they just don't know how. All they have to do is try real hard to get rid of their emotional feelings first. Then they would be able to forgive and love others. Love is the key to your happiness. Please don't throw it away. If you do, you will lock yourselves out of love and happiness.

God's Love for Us

When Jesus Christ was on earth, all the sinners and tax collectors came very close to him so they can listen to his preaching. These people came because they were outcasts. Jesus Christ was teaching about God's kingdom where he was forgiving people for their sins, healing, and saving lives not only from death but also for living a good and meaningful life. If you never hear or read the Word of God, if you never step foot in a church, I want you to know that Jesus still loves you, and his arms are wide open to welcome and to hug you. His hands are upon you. Open your hearts today to receive his warm welcome. By whatever means, I urge you to make an effort as God's creation and a human being to come closer to God. His message today for you is to make it absolutely clear to you that you understand that he loves you. His love for us is endless and has no limit and no other love can compare to. Know that it's impossible to love anybody else if you don't love God first; his love has to be in you. Brothers and sisters, God is love, and love is God. It's essential to the nature of God. We can't love God if we don't love one another. God's love is the only love that will not break your heart and turn away from you because it never fails. Let us love one another, for love is from God. Anybody who doesn't know how to love doesn't know God. He's nothing but love. It's imperative that we love one another because anyone who knows how to love has been born of God and knows God, but those who hate don't know God.

> God sent his one and only son Jesus Christ
> into the world that we might live through him.
> (1 John 4:7–9)

God really truly loves us. All we need to do is to understand and know that he does. If we don't have an assurance of God's love, our relationships and marriages with our partners or spouses won't last long, and it's a fact. There's no better love than the love of our Heavenly Father has for us as his children. His love can heal, transform lives, and free all sinners. His affection for us is limitless. He's a loving father who will always love us no matter what. We need to open our doors and allow his love to warm us, free us, change us, heal us, and lead us to the right path. We should never forget to pray before we eat, before going to bed, and when we wake up in the morning so we can keep his blessing upon us.

Brothers and sisters, we use the word *love* often to define things and people that we like and care about. More importantly, we talk about our love for our children, husbands, wives, partners just to name a few. Unfortunately, our love doesn't last forever because of differences, economical problems, death, and disappointment that come with such love. Divine and forever love is serve to us on a silver platter, and we turn away from it, a type of love that will never die nor disappoint us, which is the love of our creator, Jesus Christ. He did not give his life or went through what he went through to STOP caring for us. His unconditional love for us has no limit and no end. His love is free for whoever seeks it, and it never fails. Acknowledge God. Give him his place in your life, and know that he truly loves you forever. Let us live our lives in love so God can live in us. God is nothing but love. He loves us dearly. Most of us are aware of that but still have doubts about it.

As God's children, here's how much he loves us.

- God's love is unchanged and can transforms us.
- God's love comes with no expiration date.
- God's love comforts us.
- God's love teaches us to love one another.
- God's love protect us from evil.
- God's love blessed us with the Holy Spirit.
- God's love is revealed to us through Jesus Christ his only begotten son.

- God's love breaks chains, unties knots, and breaks all barriers.

Many of us day by day doubt this pure and true love because of bad past experience that we had with other people in relationships or marriages, leaving us with broken hearts with doubts on love, making us think, *Why would the Lord choose to love us when everyone else hate us?* Even our poor choices can make us think like that also. Let me tell you something, we don't earn God's love by behaving or acting only in a good and positive way. He loves all his children, and we can understand that when he demonstrated the greatest act of love when his only begotten son, Jesus Christ, died on the cross for us. We no longer have to seek for true love. It's given to us freely. It's very important that in our prayers, we ask the Lord our father to show us how we can reflect his love to others in our lives. Be aware that nothing or nobody has the power to change the love that God has for us. They can't buy it, and they cannot tell him otherwise. His love is very different from ours as his being is different from our being. The proverbs and the stories in the Bible tell us the kind of love that God has for us. In fact, it even says that God is love; therefore, these scripture quotes can really help us understand God's love for us. God is not mean or evil. He's not looking to punish us when we do wrong. Matter of fact, his love is identified by grace, understanding, and forgiveness. Since God loves us so much, we should also love one another, and that's the way it should be. If you haven't had a relationship with God, now is the time. He wants to have one with you so you can know what his love is all about. I know some of you have been wondering or asked yourselves that question, "Does God really love me?" Circumstances in life make you think like that, but it's okay. The doubt that you have comes from your surroundings, family members, friends, coworkers, lovers, even your children, etc. They probably let you down. You feel as though the whole world just crushes you or positions itself against you at times. With all these imperfections, your hearts become very cold; therefore, you wonder if God really could possibly love you.

So how can we really know if God loves us? The Bible is the only source that reveals the love that the Lord has for us, but show it in the most incredible way.

For example,

* Many of us, as human beings, or creation of God are very confused about who God really is because of all these religions (one God and one million religions) just to create confusion. Religions will not save you, but God will. Jesus Christ came to earth to communicate and to display that God is love.
* All sinners must be judged, but because of God indecipherable love, he chooses to send his only begotten son, Jesus Christ, to die in our place, be judged so we could be forgiven. If this isn't love, I don't know what it is.

> For God so loved the world, so he gave his only begotten son, that whoever believes in him should not perish, but have ever lasting life. (John 3:16)

God loves you very much. Please love him back by acknowledging and praying to him, by believing in him, by loving your brothers and sisters unconditionally, and by treating others the way that you would want them to treat you. May God bless you.

Self-Love

When does someone love himself or herself? Well, first thing to know is that loving yourself is personal. Loving yourself is learning how to forgive yourself, how to care about yourself, and how to tolerate yourself. Loving yourself is also watching what you're drinking and eating, overall what you're putting in your body. When you are aware of what kind of nutrition that you're nourishing your body with, that's when you have the right mind-set and a positive attitude toward yourself. You are the second one after God who deserves your love, affection, and attention before you can share them with anyone else in the whole world. As much as you think others deserve them, know that you need them first, and they belong to you. You cannot be sharing and not living any for yourself no matter what.

When you think and act in such way, you're just liking and respecting yourself (awareness). That's exactly what you call a positive state of mind. That's a real boost of your self-esteem, self-worth, and self-love. It's imperative to be gentle with yourself so you can act the same way toward others.

Here are thirteen elements of Vautoir's wall of good intentions that I'm sharing with you so you can love yourself.

- Think like you love yourself.
- Talk like you love yourself.
- Act like you love yourself.
- See things like you love yourself.
- Understand things like you love yourself.
- Go places like you love yourself.
- Choose your friends like you love yourself.
- Choose your wife or husband like you love yourself.
- Choose your partner like you love yourself.
- Walk like you love yourself.
- Breathe like you love yourself.
- Have fun like you love yourself, period.
- Enjoy being with yourself.

When you love and care about yourself, you just secure your happiness and enjoy life. Thereby, you will leave behind the past, the drama, the stress, and all other negative feelings that come in life's package and your surroundings. Trust me, you will find enough happiness to share with others, enough to feed your mind, body, and soul in a healthy way. Know that the fact that somebody loves you doesn't give you the right to sacrifice your self-love. Learn to love yourself enough to let your surroundings and society that you're part of what you will and will not tolerate from them. Learn to live your life for you, not for anyone else; know that you are unique, and you're your own person. Learn to please yourself first before you can please anybody else, and the most important person is you, not someone else. God gives you your precious life. Take good care of it. Believe in yourself. Know who you are, where you want to go, and what you want to accomplish in life; know your purpose and let people talk. I believe I can, with determination, can accomplish greatness. We are living in a world that wants us to believe otherwise about ourselves so knowing who we are, what we want, and where we want to go is the greatest accomplishment ever. First and foremost, it's a must to love yourselves, to believe in yourselves, and to care about yourselves; then only then you won't harm yourselves, kill yourselves, or commit suicide because only people who love and care about themselves won't take their lives away, and it's a fact. Be aware. There is no better love than self-love. In that case, you are licensed to say "me, myself, and I" without being selfish. It's okay. Learn to treat yourselves right and respectfully. By doing so, you will live a healthier and happier life forever after, I guarantee you.

Therefore, in order to achieve all the above, you must put God first in everything that you do and in every decision that you're making. Overall, God's first, and you're second, and there's no other way. On the other hand, do not forget to put yourself first than anyone else. Let's say when it comes to me, I fall in love with myself, I'm crazy about myself, and can't live without myself. It seems a little bit weird, isn't it? Well not really, I feel as though that we should all throw a party to celebrate our unique way and not to feel weird, ashamed, or embarrassed by it. Brothers and sisters, I guarantee you in your lifetime; if you care, love, and accept yourselves for who you are, you will drop all the heavy weights that you've been carried on your back for so long and feel free like a bird. Such self-value will not come to you and you will not find it through your friends, money, and influence; you can only find it through yourselves and through yourselves only. And never feel guilty when you position yourselves first. It's a sacred right. Trust and believe when you love, respect, value, and care about yourselves, it's because you understand that you're just important as anybody else, period. If you really care and love yourselves, it's also very important to learn how to forgive yourselves; and by doing so, you will be able to forgive others. Sinners as we are, if God didn't forgive us by his grace and have compassion for us, this world would be no more because too many evil people on this earth.

Life is unpredictable, full of problems and troubles. They will always be present on our path and in our lives, and there's nothing we can do about it; therefore, be easy on yourselves and others. Love yourselves and others. Care about yourselves and other people. And more importantly, share with others, and God will bless you in so many ways. Acts 20:35 states that "in everything I did, I showed you that by this kind of hard work we must help the weak, remembering the words the Lord Jesus himself said: It is more blessed to give than to receive" which means that there's joy and happiness in the act of giving when it's done with pure motive or when you give with all your heart. Please remember to give what you like and want, not what you don't want or consider as trash, thanks. Your state of mind has to lay on you are somebody; therefore, you have an obligation to be one and act like one. Hugging and embracing yourselves is priceless for a love that will never betray you or break your heart. It's a very powerful and unbreakable relationship when you fall in love with yourself. No matter what happens in the past, no matter what you get involved in, no matter how much wrong you did, you still can change and become a better person. God loves you.

I know that some of you think very little of yourselves or have very low self-esteem—I'm nobody, I hate myself or my life, I'm worthless etc. We have a tendency of judging ourselves when we make a simple mistake or did something wrong. We think that we're not good enough and chose to be very hard on ourselves instead of appreciating ourselves for who we really are. Loving ourselves through our mistakes is forgiving and giving ourselves a second chance because everybody deserves one. Be proud of yourselves, believe in yourselves, and see yourselves for the person that you are not for what others see you or want you to be. Being original and real is way much better than being fake. Don't be like Donald J. Trump. You are somebody, you have your values, character, integrity, and dignity; know that they are not for sale. They're the only things that you will take with you to the grave, and know your purpose. In life, place yourself first before everybody else but God, and everything else will fall into place. No one can pour from an empty bottle. Make sure that yours have something in it so you can serve others. Believe in yourself when others don't. It will make you a winner not a loser. Love yourself when no one else loves you, and that's when you will meet with true love. One thing that you have to know is that when it comes to human beings, there's no superior nor inferior. You can only be inferior if you allow yourself to be. Never forget to smile and be happy, and that's the only precious gift that you can give to your health. No need to try to be perfect, it's unrealistic. Only God is, but always try your best to do what you do best. In order to be strong and to stay strong, we have to have the ability to embrace life with all its children (problems and troubles).

Believe it or not, they will always come and knock at our doors or chase us around even though we didn't invite them or look for them as we can see they need no license or permit from nobody to act. Regardless of how other people see you, feel about you, things they say behind your back, what they think of you shouldn't STOP you from loving and believing in yourself. When you believe in yourself, you become strong and solid; therefore, no stick or stone can break your bones. Most people are not fair in this world, but we always blame the world when it has nothing to do with it; we always say, "The world is not fair." It's not the world. It's us who don't make an effort to treat others fairly or the way that they deserve to be treated. Loving yourselves unconditionally will give you real power to pull others from an invisible string to come into your life who will love you with no hesitation, no conditions, and no contract. Not everyone in life will understand you like you, care about you; but for those who do, they will never forget you. When we love ourselves, it brings lots of positive things or positive vibes into it, even the unexpected. It is way much better to hold on to the remote control of your lives or hide it in a safe place so no one can control you but God and you only. Let the past be the past and take action now so you can turn your lives around; otherwise, you will be living your lives in the past for the rest of your lives, very unhealthy.

Here are seven elements to succeed from Vautoir's wall of good intentions that I'm sharing with you.

- Do not limit yourselves ever. Always try your best to reach higher!
- Success will not be served to you. Only determination will give you a free ride and drop you to it!
- Be ambitious and dream big!
- Never put what you can do now for tomorrow. It doesn't belong to you. You never know what can happen.
- Push yourselves to the extreme without looking back!
- The harder you work, the better chance you have to achieve greatness.
- Put yourself in service of others. Be humble!

Don't let anybody put your down by telling you that you're not good enough or smart enough. Anybody can become successful; all you need is determination. Yes, it's real take sometimes, but it's possible. You can do better, work hard, and improve yourself day by day so you can get closer and closer to your dream because success demands great effort, and it doesn't come overnight. All successful people work very hard to get where they at one way or the other; therefore, don't hate no one for what they have. Instead, use your brain to gain your own. Nothing is easy in life. But if you want to reach higher, make sure that you learn how to fly first so you don't break your wings because if they are broken, you won't be able to fly, and you will be stuck in one place. As long as you have the desire, hunger, and the ambition to be successful, you will. All you have to do is look for a jumping cable and jump-start the power within you to achieve it. Nobody can be successful without these three components: desire, hunger, and ambition. When you love yourself, you're just protecting your own well-being and happiness. And when you find yourself in that state of mind, you will automatically know your needs and wants, and you will never settle for less than what you deserve, which is also a form of success. That's a very good and healthy lifestyle with no stress, no anxiety, and no depression. It's inevitable that you just boost your entire system with the conviction (by doing so, will help you live a better and fulfilled life). Remember, brothers and sisters, that your mental well-being is also as important as your physical well-being so take good care of them.

Here are nineteen elements from Vautoir's wall of good intentions so you can be in control of your life that I'm sharing with you.

- Look for anything that will make you smile and hug yourself from time to time.
- Be yourself and be special in your unique way. It's okay to be different!
- Always try to accomplish great things, and when you do, be proud and give yourself a pat on the back. It's okay!
- Be fatally allergic to negativity. Avoid drama. Positivity is the way to go.
- Be unstoppable, live your life to the fullest, and let nothing or anybody STOP you from doing so.
- Surround yourself with real people while keeping the fake ones away from you.
- Never compare yourself to anyone else. You are you, and you will always be you, no one else. No matter how hard you try to be somebody else, it will never happen; you can only be you!
- Make sure you get rid of all toxic people in your life. For real, anyone who makes you feel less than awesome and beautiful doesn't deserve to be your friend, partner, husband, wife, or family member.
- Nourish your body with healthy foods and drinks so you can live and die healthy.
- Never doubt yourself for one second. Follow your passion. Know that you can do anything if you put your mind to it!
- Treat others with respect, fairness, understanding, and compassion so they can treat you the same.
- Do to others what you want them to do to you, reproduction!
- Be grateful. See what you have, not what you don't, and thank God for it; it doesn't matter how big or small it is!

- Don't be afraid to say NO. Know what's good and what's bad for you. Choosing to say NO to certain things and people is being smart!
- Don't think for a second that you can please everybody. If you do, you're nothing but a fool!
- When things are not working the way they should and you are going through hard times, call the Lord. He got your back.
- Let no one talk to you in any kind of way!
- Make sure that you learn something new every day. If you don't, someone else will, and that person will get smarter and smarter than you. (My cousin Jean Fanes Snare taught me that.)

When you learn to love and care about yourself, especially your well-being, you will learn to take others with heart and to treat them with respect and fairly. Such motivation doesn't only give you a high regard for your own well-being but also for others' wellbeing; it's all about love. Another thing, when you fall in love with yourself, you're communicating with love, and love communicates with you. And such love is unbreakable, untouchable, and unstoppable. Love yourself so you can live a better, happier, and healthier life.

Self-Confidence

As they say, "Self-confidence is a feeling of trust in one's abilities, qualities and judgement." It's also a feeling of belief, if I may say, because when you believe in yourself, you trust your own judgement and abilities to decide and do things in a positive manner. It's also a feeling that pushes you to think highly and value yourself and feel worthy, no matter how others see you, what they think about you or your imperfections. I know that many of you are living a nightmare such as stress, self-doubt, depression, and anxiety which are the result of having fear to achieve greatness or to be successful. Mostly these fears or negative feelings are teamed up with a lack of self-confidence that gives them power to drown your self-esteem. We all need our self-esteem so we can cope with what's going on in our lives, especially in this world that we're living in. And that's exactly why we need to believe in ourselves (self-confidence) so we can jumpstart our self-esteem. For example, you are driving your car, and it died on you. You find out that it's your battery that went dead. What would be your first reaction? You would open your trunk and look for your jumping cable if you have one and ask another driver for a jump, right. Well, to let you know, there's no difference when it comes to your self-esteem, self-confidence, values, beliefs, and understanding, etc. We have to boost them from time to time.

Self-confidence will give us the ability to think positively and to be able to compete so; therefore, whatever we put our minds to, we can do. It's vital that you stay in competition with yourself for yourself only, not with anybody else. With such state of mind, you will easily meet with Mr. Success and Mr. Greatness that will shake your hand and say "please to meet you." Without self-confidence, we cannot be in competition with ourselves, and we will only be able to see the shadow of these two elements that I've mentioned above passing by. Understand that the understanding and the negative attitudes that some people have toward themselves and other people is the toxic package that they carry with them wherever they go. It came exactly from the way they were raised and treated as children. Many children in this world unfortunately were told by their parents, family members, or the people or friends that they were good for nothing, useless. They will never achieve anything in their life, or worse, they compare them to other no-good people that they don't even know or heard bad news about. These kinds of parents don't even care if their children make it or not; and as a result, the only message that the children pull from such negative behaviors is having low self-esteem, low self-confidence, and fear to fail, which is very sad and unfortunate. Having such negative feelings about themselves don't just manifest in a sense of being worthless; it also shows its true color in action whenever they try to do or accomplish something. In their state of mind, they know and believe a head of time that they're going to fail. Thereof, demanding and desirable work is extremely difficult, even absent. So when the negative or the distracting feeling reaches such level, it becomes very serious because they position themselves before danger.

They will fail mostly in anything they try to do even though they have the will such as relationships, marriages, businesses, etc., and will be a failure no matter how hard they try. They live with a state of mind that is telling them what they used to hear from their negative people in their surroundings by saying to themselves: I'm not going to make it. I'm going to fail. It's not going to last, and I can't do it. And that's exactly why they say "be careful for what you wish for." Therefore, feeling so pessimistic will weaken them from accomplishing anything worthwhile. And the worse scenario of all this is that they hate challenge or competition, and anything in that nature appears to be too hard for them to take part of or to do. But believe it or not, they're not afraid of failure because they expected it. It becomes a great accomplishment for them because they already knew the outcome (believing is seeing).

When you think negative, negative things and actions will take place; but when you think positive, positive things and actions will surface, and it's a fact. You are what you think you are as they say. So from this logical theory, we can clearly understand that when self-confidence is not present, it can be very difficult for us to take any chances and risks in life when life is all about these two components. Please don't let fear, failure, and chaos define your lives and your future. You can do better, and you deserve better. Trust and believe that we all have qualities that would inspire others. All we have to do is seek for them by running after them and catching them so we can put them to use, and they are qualities that others would admire and be fired up by. Self-confidence is a quality that nobody can minimize. It's vital that we value and believe in ourselves because no one else will.

Sincerely, when you're a self-confident person, you inspire others to do the same. It can be your family members, your friends, your coworkers, your partners, your spouses, your students, your teachers, your children, your customers, and even your bosses. When people believe in you, they place their trust in you so their confidence can hold your hand and walk with you toward success so in reality, self-confidence can be learned and taught. Therefore, while building your confidence, you can also build other people's self-confidence as well, both works. Self-confident people don't have to look far for positivity. It will be there for you automatically. Self-confidence will help you to believe in yourselves and open your eyes so you can see that you have abilities to do and accomplish things. And such positive feeling will also help you to determine the level of your self-confidence. When you know the level of your self-confidence, you will understand clearly where you stand and in what ways you lack of confidence, which I'll talk about later.

Self-confidence takes time to be build. It's not a week or two-weeks thing; it's a day-by-day process. The good news though is that you can do it. It's achievable. All you need is courage, good will, determination, and passion to carry things through like a real soldier. The wonderful thing about such vision is that it works for both entities, the same energy it takes you to build your self-confidence; it will also work for your success. You kill two birds with one stone. After such hard work, your self-confidence will cross the bridge of solid achievement with you so finally you can take a deep breath and smile. I also once suffered from this disease called "fear to fail," and that's exactly what held me back so I couldn't move forward. It's something that each one of us, as human beings, face to some degree, believe it or not. Once we start believing in ourselves, we can easily overcome it. When you believe in yourselves, that's the moment you start working on your self-confidence without thinking about failure but success, and that's exactly what I have been doing. Now I can say with no hesitation, for me failure is no more. It's dead and buried; therefore, I become fearless and can easily pursue my dream. So all I did is break the bones of fear by embracing self-confidence and become free. I have no doubts in my mind now that one day, I'm going to be very successful and find myself on the other side of life. And this fearlessness will soon fuel my helicopter of success so I can fly around the world. When you believe in yourself, you know you're worthy, and others respect you. Such belief will make you think highly of yourself because it will boost your self-confidence and your self-esteem to put you in control of your life. Therefore, for taking control and be in control, you're cleaning and detailing your self-image and improve your competence.

Here are fifteen elements of Vautoir's wall of good intentions to keep you in control of your life that I'm sharing with you.

- Be in good mood at all times
  Be in good mood at all times no matter what. It will keep your heart smiling, and you will stay healthy.
- Feel good about yourself
  When you feel good about yourself, you will stay happy. You will love and take good care of yourself. You matter.
- Think positively about yourself
  Take a good look of yourself in the mirror and ask yourself some valuable questions so you can start your day with positive affirmations.
- Bury all negative thoughts
  Thinking negative about yourself is not an option. Kill all negative thoughts so you can make great things happen in your life. Negative thinking is nothing but a bunch of mosquitoes trying to suck on your energy and at the same time playing violin into your brain to distract you.
- Know yourself well
  When you know yourself pretty well, doubt keeps its distance.
- Put your positivism in action
  Acting positively is way much greater than just thinking positively. Think and act positively. Show others respect. Let your actions talk for you, and soon enough, you'll start to notice a big difference on how others treat you.
- Show some gratitude
  In order to show some gratitude, first and foremost, you have to be content to what you have. Through gratitude, you can improve the quality of your life and the life of others, especially your loved ones.

- Improve yourself image
  Improve your self-image by being kind with others and be generous with what you have by helping those in need. Such behavior will send you and other people some fire work to let you know that you're a good person which indeed will make you feel good about yourself.
- Live by principles
  Build your life on principles. Without them, your life will have no direction. I know many of you believe in principles and don't live by them. It's a must that you live and act on them for your own good and your surroundings.
- Communicate kindly
  By speaking kindly to others, it will have a big impact on how they perceive you. People will respect you and will want to do good by you. And that's exactly why they say "kindness is contagious."
- Think highly of yourself
  When you think highly of yourself, you will feel better about yourself. Please don't take it to the extreme. If you do, you will, in a sense, think that you're superior of others when you're not. Keep your head high and walk tall.
- Set your goals
  Analyze and study your goals just to make sure that they're achievable. If you fail, it's okay. Don't give up. Try again until you're succeed. And when you do, feel good about yourself and be proud.
- Be hungry for knowledge
  The more knowledgeable you are, the better. Knowledge is power. Do some research, go to college, and communicate with knowledgeable people. Read educational books. These are some of the strategies to empower yourself with knowledge.
- Take steps to accomplish something
  Don't sit on your butt all day playing video games or watching TV. They will not bring anything good into your life. It doesn't matter how small or big what you have to do.

Most importantly, do something positive that will make people talk about you in a positive way. Know yourself, believe in yourself, and let people talk.

- Lack of self-confidence

   When you have a lack of self-confidence, you automatically have a low self-esteem. And when you position yourself in the basket of these two elements, you will feel unwanted, unloved, incompetent, and worthless.

It's true that sometimes we don't feel good about ourselves, but when we embrace and hold on to low self-esteem and don't let go, it will bring on your path a lack of self-confidence which is a big problem that can destroy your happiness and have a negative effect on your mental health. What is low self-esteem? It's the negative opinions that we have of ourselves or the way that we think, and the way that we think dominates our opinions. When our self-esteem is low, we tend to think negative and act negatively; therefore, we will position ourselves or our lives in a more open window where we can easily fall and break our necks. Low self-esteem is caused by a shock of electricity or negative messages that children have received about themselves from their surroundings. Unfortunately, all these negative messages or shock of electricity stay with them through their entire lives. These poor children grow up with these negative feelings and carry them on to their own children. It's a vicious cycle. They're stuck on negative thinking while other children are reaching very high to accomplish greatness. When you have a lack of self-confidence, you're just practicing social distance with your surroundings and the rest of the world. Such attitude will prevent you from trying new things that would allow you to move forward. You might think that you're safe when you're lonely, but that's not the case because loneliness is sadness. Avoiding challenges and difficult situations don't make you safe. It just makes you lonely. You can't spend the rest of your lives avoiding challenges and people. That's shaking up and waking up your fear and doubts that have the power to kill your self-confidence. And with this happening, it will bring you all the wrong things such as stress, depression, and anxiety. You will also develop some deadly habits like getting high and become alcoholic as a way of coping. It's not smart at all to put your life and your future in such destructive path. It's a very poor self-image.

You probably have a little voice in your head that's telling you that you deserve all the bad things in the world—your life sucks, and you can't do better. The time is now to say no to your negative thinking and start thinking and acting positively. When you have healthy self-esteem, you believe in yourself, and you have self-confidence, without a doubt in my mind that you will be positive about your abilities and have a better approach to life in general. We also have, around the world, a bunch of highly educated brothers and sisters that suffer from a lack of confidence. But one way or the other, at some point in their lives, they allowed negative thoughts and bad situations to walk all over their self-esteem and self-confidence, and day by day, it has continued to affect their success and performance. Such anomaly affects also their ability to reach their full potential, unfortunately. These brothers and sisters feel joyful in their little comfort zone simply because there's no big risk or failure there. They feel safe. The truth is if you don't allow yourselves to make mistakes and people to criticize you and you're not willing to take some risks, it will be very difficult for you to grow and strive. But most importantly, there are some valuable lessons in life that you won't be able to learn because we learn by our mistakes and criticism of others. A lack of confidence will hold you back and can even stop you from communicating in a positive way with others.

Here are four ways to overcome your lack of confidence from Vautoir's wall of good intentions that I'm sharing with you!

- Live in the present
    When you live your life in the present, not the past, you will make better choices and better decisions for your future and your career.
- Learn to please yourself
    Don't live to please others but yourself. By doing so, you will know your needs and wants before anyone else. It's the best way to disable all other thoughts that put others before you.

- STOP all negative thinking

    When you don't think negatively about yourself, you're making room for positive thinking. Remember, you are what you think you are.
- Be humble

    Put yourself in service of others, especially the less fortunate. Be a servant, love, and be kind and respectful to others; the reproduction of such attitude and behavior will be worthwhile.

Here are eleven elements of Vautoir's wall of good intentions, so you can boost your confidence, that I'm sharing with you!

- Know that you're important, and you have values.
- Step away from drama, negative things, and people.
- Make positive friends.
- Make time for yourself.
- Take it easy on yourself. Stop blaming yourself for every little thing.
- Take time to plan your future even though you don't know what it will bring and when it's going to shine.
- Spend time only with people who understand you, respect you, love and care about you.
- Forgive yourself and know that your mistakes can't define you as a person and for who you are.
- Challenge your negative thoughts at all times.
- Do things that can only bring you happiness.
- Know that God loves you. It's a must for you to communicate with him day and night so you can receive his blessings.

Self-Compassion

Self-compassion simply means to treat yourself right and providing yourself with the kind of love, protection, acceptance, and safety that you deserve. It's also a way to pass the soccer ball to yourself and kick it real hard so you can tear up the net of pain and suffering and score big time. When you have compassion for yourself, you will automatically have it for others. Take a moment of your time and think for a quick second how compassion feels like. It's a very juicy feeling in a sense of making you feel good and proud. In the other hand, if you have no compassion for yourself, you will have none for others. If you ignore a beggar on the street, my common sense will tell me right away that you not a compassionate person so it's impossible to feel compassion for the kind of life that he's living and what he went through in his life. There's no doubt that when you're a compassionate person, you take other people's pain and suffering at heart and always try to find a way to help. And that's exactly why the word *compassion* means to be in pain with, to suffer with, and to share with, to understand the situation of such. Anyway, that's how I see and understand the word *compassion*.

Self-compassion also means taking action by defending, protecting, and motivating ourselves by saying "no" to each and every one out there who takes pleasure in hurting us in anyway and also by taking advantage of us. We have to install our fence or our divided line with a big STOP sign which will give us a chance to fulfill what we need spiritually, mentally, and physically. self-compassion works. I say it works because it works for me. I have seen the benefits of it in my life. Self-compassion makes me a better person and keeps me righteous and gives me light to do the right thing even though my life was captivated by poverty and hardship. It also keeps me on a positive path and showed me its benefit when it comes to well-being. I always say to myself, "Things are going to get better. I'm going to make it no matter what." Self-compassion keeps me going and changes my life for the better. It really makes me the person that I am today. Everybody's problem is my problem, can't see anyone suffering, good hearted person, love and care about everybody. That's who I am, a compassionate person, and so does my wife Yvonie.

She takes pleasure in giving than receiving. We think alike, and I really believe that God puts us together for a purpose, and not only that God put us together but he also created us for each other; that's exactly why we're so much in love. I am not bragging, people. I'm just telling the truth so please let the truth be told because if I don't tell you, you won't know, and you would be still in the dark. Self-compassion freezes me from being a murderer, a drug dealer, a thief, and a rapist. It also keeps me on the right track of life, which is God's side. Therefore, self-compassion is not only about being kind, respectful, understanding, and caring; it's also about common sense and good judgement. If you haven't practiced self-compassion yet, what are you waiting for? I promise you that you will be free of all negative feelings just like myself, try it. Self-compassion will guide and help you so you can have a happier and healthier relationship with yourself, your spouse, your partner, your friends, your coworkers, your family, etc.

Other Benefits of Self-Compassion!

- It will increase your confidence.
- It will drown all personal doubts that you might have about yourself.
- It will magnify self-worth.
- It will bring kindness, understanding, respect, and love to you on a silver platter.
- It will help you understand that personal failure is part of life.
- It will knock out all your negative emotions.

Let me tell you something, the same compassion, respect, forgiveness and love that you give without hesitation to others and your surroundings can also be given to you, by you, and for you. If you can do it for other people, you can do it for yourself too. Love God, love yourself, and love others. And may the Holy Spirit guide you through your life for ever and ever.

CONCLUSION

Do not stop dreaming, and dream big when you do. Do everything in your power to make your dreams come true. Yes, it will take sometimes, but it's not impossible. It's achievable. Be aware, a man without a dream is a fried fish with a fried brain. Be a hungry dog for success, and I promise you, one day, you'll find something to bite on. Do like I did. Go to YouTube University, and I guarantee you that you can learn a lot from it. Have some role models into your life. Let some positive people bring some good vibes into your life. I have some golden hearts as my role models—Oprah Winfrey, Ellen DeGeneres, Martin Luther King Jr., Steve Harvey, just to name a few.

Do not focus on what people think or say about you. Focus on you and you alone. Stay away from losers, low lives, and drama queens, better to surrender yourselves with knowledgeable and educated people for a better you. Don't let nobody control your life. The remote control of your life has to be in God's hands, not a family member, not a friend, not your wife or husband nor a coworker. The last name of this world is trouble. They will always look for you even though you never look for them, and there's no way to hide when they come. The best you can do is never give up no matter what. Be unstoppable, undeniable, and always keep it real. Look only forward, and that's the only way you will meet with success. Let the past be the past. Let it rest for the sake of your health and happiness. Be a servant, be respectful, and adopt kindness so you can make an impact on other people's lives. Believe in yourselves (confidence), and it will take you on the path of your journey. Never give up. If you do, you become a loser, not a winner. A loser loses, and a winner wins.

And that's the greatest feeling ever, when you win. Use wisdom and compassion wherever you go and in everything that you do. People will love you for it. Be grateful for what you have, and STOP complaining about what you don't have; such mentality will take you no further than your nose. Complaining doesn't change the situation. Only determination can turn things around. Life is not easy, but you can ease it by doing what's best for you. God bless you, God bless America, and God bless the world.

ABOUT THE AUTHOR

My name is Bianka Paul, and I am Jean Vautoir Paul's daughter. It's an honor for me to write about the author who happens to be my father. One would say that it is natural for a child to speak positively about their parents because it is their right to do so, but my father deserves it. I have watched him, with sustained attention, be the best father he can be. Whether it comes down to communicating or taking actions, he has always done his best. And he has never given up on his dreams even though he has failed many times. I cannot count how many times my father has talked about publishing a book even when no one could picture how it was going to happen. My father is a visionary thinker and very courageous. He is selfless when it comes to the people he holds dear, and he is an educational and kindhearted man. Many may perceive him differently because they may not understand his character. I watched him be humiliated by those who believed he won't make it, but he keeps going and believes in what he believes. I have watched him be silent and pretend that everything is okay, and not once has he complained. As his daughter, I want nothing more than for him to finally accomplish his dreams, including educating, inspiring, and uplifting as many people as he can through his writing by opening their eyes to his world. If you ask me, I am proud of him, and always will be.

CPSIA information can be obtained
at www.ICGtesting.com
Printed in the USA
JSHW050326220222
23173JS00001B/54